The Tao
of
Quitting Smoking

Written by Joseph P. Weaver
Edited by Gary Toushek
Illustrated by Bettina Johnson

The Tao of Quitting Smoking

First published as *Nic the Habit.*

Published by Hats Off Books™
610 East Delano Street, Suite 104, Tucson, Arizona 85705 U.S.A.
www.hatsoffbooks.com

International Standard Book Number: 1-58736-315-1
Library of Congress Control Number: 2004103948

Publisher's Cataloging-in-Publication
(Provided by Quality Books, Inc.)

Weaver, Joseph P.
The tao of quitting smoking / written by Joseph P. Weaver ; edited by Gary Toushek ; illustrated by Bettina Johnson.
p. cm.
First published as Nic the habit.
LCCN 2004103948
ISBN 1-58736-315-1

1. Tobacco habit. 2. Nicotine. 3. Smoking. I. Toushek, Gary. II. Johnson, Bettina. III. Weaver, Joseph P. Nic the habit. IV. Title.

HV5733.W34 2004 362.29'6
QBI33-2021

QUIT
BECAUSE
YOU
CAN

Dedicated to my mother
Eris Weaver Miller

INTRODUCTION

It is said that the teacher comes when the student is ready! Congratulations! This is your first step toward a new life without smoking. In this book, I will give you all the tools necessary for you to become a nonsmoker for the rest of your life. The book is structured unlike any other on the market. Not only will this book help you end your addiction to nicotine, but it will also help you discover how to regain control of your life.

The Tao of Quitting Smoking is a book about self-discovery, reaching within, and discovering the reasons you allowed yourself to become addicted to a substance. This is the key element to freeing yourself of nicotine, a powerful, addictive drug. With self-awareness and the knowledge presented in this book, you will have all the elements you need to say goodbye to tobacco products forever.

Before writing this book, I smoked two to three packs of cigarettes a day for more than seventeen years. Each year, I made an attempt to quit but was unsuccessful. In this book, I will share with you my first experience with cigarettes at the age of fifteen—and how, seventeen years later, it was possible for me to say goodbye to cigarettes forever. I was able to not only quit smoking, but also lost more than eighty pounds in the process.

My passage to awareness and freedom began during an escapade to Nepal, and later Tibet. There I learned that my addictions to nicotine and food were more than just cravings. I began to notice other patterns in my life that that I did not like. I was also addicted to coffee, sex, food, people, work, and drama. Being in a foreign country for more than a month, with a limited amount of money and no friends, there were many lonely days and nights when I did not speak a word to anyone; the culture, the people, and the language were all very new and strange to me. At times, the only thing that I could do was to go inward and explore my soul. Traveling alone in a foreign country forced me to take time out from my hectic world and slow down.

By going inward, I realized that I was depressed, had low self-esteem, and was not happy with my life. Nicotine was a drug for me to forget about how I felt inside. Nicotine was working as an antianxiety and antidepressant. So when I felt stressed, I popped a cigarette into my life. Before I knew it, I couldn't function without a cigarette. I became a slave to the drug: nicotine before eating, after eating, with coffee, after coffee, before sex, after sex, while on the phone, when talking to people, when outside. I was controlled by a substance that was slowly killing me. I wanted to quit, but I did not know how to survive without nicotine.

Fear drove my inability to make the decision to stop—and never go back. The fear of failing and starting again; the fear of gaining weight when I was already too fat; the fear of not knowing how to handle the excess stress of quitting … these fears were the main reasons I continually put off quitting smoking 'til tomorrow, or next month, or not at all. Acceptance and denial were my actions. Our human nature is used to seeking pleasure and avoiding pain. That is one of the reasons drugs can be addictive.

Nicotine affects the part of the brain's chemistry that is involved in feelings, the reward system, and the ability to experience. I could never motivate myself enough to quit, and when I did, I felt so horrible and irritable that smoking was easier than quitting.

You, the reader, won't have to travel to another country to discover that the answers lie within yourself to overcome your additions to nicotine. It's all about avoiding pain and seeking pleasure—the pain/pleasure principle, which we will talk about later.

This book is structured to take you on your spiritual journey and help you re-examine the reasons you allow yourself to be a victim to nicotine. No, this book is not about blaming yourself, but rather about giving you back the control, in order to change your life. Quitting smoking is easy once you make the decision to quit.

This book is about taking control of your actions. It's about decisions and how they affect and shape your destiny. Continuing to smoke is a choice—a weak choice, but still a decision. True decisions leave no room for chance; they are not based on inactions. This book is about your truth and the ability to just say no to nicotine. Most people aren't aware that nicotine is a drug or how extremely addictive it can be. It is known to be more addictive than heroine and cocaine. But before we begin to talk about the additive properties of nicotine and the reasons we allow it to control us, we must first make an agreement between us.

Rule 1. Keep an open mind.

Rule 2. Assignments in this book can't be substituted or ignored.

Rule 3. Read this book from beginning to end. This is not the type of book where you can skip chapters or skim pages. Quitting smoking is one of the most important decisions you will make in your life, so please take your time and don't rush this book along. Your subconscious will try to get you to stop reading this book; ignore it! Complete what you start!

Rule 4. Focus on quitting, not on all the times you have quit before and failed. Don't focus on how much weight you might gain. I will help you with quitting and not gaining weight.

Rule 5. My main goal is to help you quit smoking using your own inner strength. Occasionally, you may feel that I am a bit strong in my choice of words. Or you may not like the way I express myself. Ignore your mind's attempt to find the negatives or to stop reading this book; this is normal. Just relax! Remember that it is easier to make the choice to continue to smoke. It takes absolutely no action. Your mind will seek to give up in order to not experience the pain from quitting.

Rule 6. You must be serious about wanting to quit smoking. Why do you want to quit? You need to answer that question. Do you want to be healthier? Is it because of the cost? Is it because you are sick and tired of being addicted to tobacco products? Think about why you truly want to quit—and if you are serious about quitting, then I am happy for you!

Read on … If you are not ready and are just checking this book out, then please, put it aside until you are prepared to give at least a 50 percent effort. Honestly, quitting smoking is not as difficult as you may think. Don't worry about all the times you attempted to quit but failed. The past is just the past! Don't worry about your willpower to stop smoking. I will help you with everything you need in order to say goodbye to cigarettes forever.

I want to note that when I talk about smoking, I am referring to all types of tobacco. Whether you smoke cigarettes, a pipe, a cigar, or even if you use snuff or chewing tobacco, it is all the same. All of those products contain nicotine, the addictive chemical that keeps you hooked on a habit. Thus, throughout this book, I may refer to smoking cigarettes, but what I am addressing are all tobacco products containing nicotine.

My main goal is not to insult you, but instead to wake you up from your addiction to nicotine and encourage you to choose health over death.

This book is about self-discovery and quitting smoking, not about writing a literary work of art. I say this because I have often bought quit-smoking books but never finished reading them because I did not enjoy the author's style of writing, or I found fault. Save that type of reasoning for novels and books of pleasure. This book is about leaning how to stay focused, stay in control, and finish what you started. It is much easier to give up and make excuses than to stay focused and not let yourself fall into traps of the conscious. So, let's begin!

Cigarette smoking kills!

I won't use euphemisms to sweeten my words or play the "politically correct" game, in order to not upset my readers. My main goal is for you to hate everything about smoking—not for you to continue living in denial about cigarettes helping you cope with stress. After reading this book, I want you to abhor everything about tobacco! There is just no other way. Believe it or not, this is the main key to becoming a nonsmoker for the rest of your life. The key is to build a strong dislike toward smoking, tobacco, and nicotine. You can't quit smoking and still be in love with the idea of smoking. Wisdom and compassion are important. We have to be smart enough to see what hurts and compassionate enough to not do it.

CHAPTER 1

No More Excuses

To quit smoking, you need to face some of the tough, hard facts that sometimes may sound a bit strong, but there are no in-betweens. Smoking has the power to kill you. What is truly mind-boggling is that you are paying the tobacco companies your hard-earned money to cause you harm. Yeah, I know you believe that it can't happen to you. As individuals, we believe we are truly an exception to life's rules. You are not, and neither am I. If you continue to smoke, you put yourself at risk, *serious* risk. Life is a risk in itself, so why complicate it with smoking? Why gamble with your health, especially if you are paying for that risk with your own money? Every day that you continue to smoke, instead of quitting, you increase your chances of developing a smoking-related illness. This is not a scare tactic. I don't want to scare you. I simply want you to wake up and realize what you are doing to yourself. Save your money for the stock market if you want to gamble.

Denial plays a big role in a smoker's life, and it helps keeps the smoker tethered to tobacco products with excuses, such as "I can quit anytime I want to" or "I'm just not ready to quit now." Excuses as to why you can't quit smoking are lame and unjustified. Nicotine has a hold on you, and you have to realize this before you begin to quit smoking. No person in their right mind would ignore all the warnings, the health risks, and the research, which shows that smoking damages your health. Even if you don't believe the research, you can't tell me that you believe smoking is beneficial to you.

Let's get serious and start right now to be truthful to yourself. You are addicted to nicotine. You must learn to be honest with yourself. It doesn't matter how many times you have attempted to quit and have failed. Failing is a part of life, and there is nothing wrong with it. No one on this planet is perfect—absolutely no one! We all fail many times in our lives, and learning from our mistakes gives us the knowledge and the strength not to repeat them. If you want to seriously quit, then you must realize that you can't successfully quit smoking while remaining blinded to your addiction. You must first make the decision to quit and plan the necessary actions to never light up another cigarette again.

CHAPTER 2

Becoming Hooked on an Image

I remember the first time I put a cigarette in my mouth; I was fifteen and innocent. Today, a nonsmoker, I ask myself why I started smoking. I remember my first cigarette vividly, recalling how horrible it felt when I took my first puff. It was my birthday, and I went riding in the park with my new bike. In my neighborhood park, I met up with a bunch of friends smoking cigarettes. My friend Tony yelled out, "Happy Birthday," and I walked over to where they were sitting. For some reason, I asked Tony if he had another cigarette. I felt older, and I wanted to celebrate. It was my birthday and I wanted to feel like a man, instead of a boy. Tony laughed and said, "Hey Joe, you don't smoke. You're just a kid."

He was just two years older, and I thought to myself, Who does he think he is? I am more a man than he is. I was great at tennis, played football, ran on the track team, studied karate, and was in decent shape. Tony did not play sports. He was out of shape and always sick, but he was more popular with girls than I was. Why? I could never understand.

Tony started smoking when he was twelve. At that age, I was still playing with my G.I. Joe and toy trucks. He was the town rebel, the guy that no one was allowed to play with. I was the average, good, neighborhood kid that everyone trusted. I was, however, getting a bit tired of that image and wanted to be more daring and not always do the "right thing," so smoking was my way into a "new Joe" who was daring and exciting.

These were some of the images that I believed cigarette smoking could help accomplish for me. I wanted to be a rebel. My urge to have a cigarette grew stronger. I again asked Tony—this time in a stronger voice—"Hey, what's up, come on, give me a cigarette!" He did, and I felt relieved. I wanted so badly to fit in and be part of the crew. Looking back, I realized that I was hooked on the image of smoking. I was brainwashed.

My inexperience with smoking became evident when I had problems lighting the match. The wind was a bit strong, and it would continually blow the match out before I could bring it up to my cigarette to light it. I must have tried six times to light that darn thing with no luck. This was the first clue that I was not a smoker. Tony said, "What a moron" and took the cigarette from me. He cuffed his hands in such a way that he blocked the wind from blowing out the match and lit it on his first attempt.

I have never felt so inadequate, yet I was a pretty confident kid growing up. To ensure that the cigarette would not burn out after it was lit, Tony took a long deep drag and handed the cigarette back to me. Just as I took it and brought it to my mouth, my friends started to laugh. I thought to myself, What the hell is wrong now? My friend Billy told me that I held the cigarette like a girl. I responded by giving him the finger. Billy took the cigarette from my mouth and proceeded to show me how a real man held it. He then imitated how I held the cigarette, and it did look a bit funny then, so I began to laugh.

I saw that there were rules to smoking, and in order to be part of the new adult clique, I learned the techniques quickly. You had to know how to light, hold, inhale, and exhale a cigarette. I was told that women smoked differently than men. I had to smoke like a man. I now began to feel cool and part of the guys' club. I knew how to light the cigarette and how to hold it correctly, and I was even shown how to strike a match with one hand, without tearing the match from the matchbook. I finally took my first puff.

You know the rest. I started to cough, got light-headed, and even felt as if I was going to throw up. I knew this could not be a good thing, but I wanted to be cool among my friends. I grew up in a town with many cliques, and I was now part of the "in" crowd, so I tried to refrain from coughing as best as I could.

I remember telling one of my friends that this crap tasted like poison. Now I knew why Tony was always coughing and spitting up phlegm. It seemed like Tony got mono or the flu every year. My subconscious told me that I was a fool for wanting to smoke. At that instant I knew I would be causing damage to my body. Fear came with that thought, and I wanted to forget about the whole smoking quest. I knew my mother would kill me if she caught me smoking, and my karate sensei would, without a doubt, kick me out of karate training. I was trained to be in control of my mind, body, and spirit. I did not have to read the surgeon general's warnings to know how harmful cigarettes were. How could something that tasted so horrible be good for you?

As you will learn from this book, cigarettes actually do contain poisons, more than two hundred known carcinogens. So in fact, it was true: I was poisoned and already knew this at fifteen. I am sure when you smoked your first cigarette it was also not a pleasant experience. It was more important for me to present the illusion to others that I was tough, cool, and not a kid anymore. My first cigarette was the rite of passage to manhood. I felt proud of myself. What a fool I was! If I had known all of the things I know today about smoking, and how it would take control of my life, I would like to think I would have never started, but I also know that to be false.

I was a bit stubborn, and I loved to try new things. For me, smoking was living on the edge. It was doing something that I knew my parents would disapprove of. I still would have smoked. Even though I felt so sick from my first puff, I took another drag, and this time inhaled deeply. I remember coughing for almost two minutes. I felt so light-headed that I had to sit down. Tony told me not to worry; I would get use to it, and he told me that smoking would put hair on my chest. Tony never mentioned that smoking causes havoc to every cell in my body and eventually causes cancer. Tony gave me his pack of cigarettes for my birthday and told me to practice. This was my first experience with smoking, and I can remember it very clearly. It wasn't long before I was hooked.

CHAPTER 3
The College Years

Smoking went on into college. I was seventeen and smoked a pack a day. Still, I did not believe I was addicted. I was into meditation, yoga, and nutrition, and I stopped going to karate classes. When people asked me how I could smoke and also be so health conscious, I would always reply, "I'm not really a smoker, I just smoke when I'm nervous, or to kill time." I must have been extremely nervous, because I also smoked when I awoke, was on the phone, before meals, after meals, and outdoors. I also smoked in my car, while drinking coffee, after drinking coffee, while watching television, before sex, and after sex. I smoked at every possible opportunity.

In college, I focused on pre-med studies and brain research. I knew the statistics about smoking and its effects on the human system. I was young and healthy, and I believed that smoking-related illnesses would never come my way. My statements of denial were: "Everyone must die of something … Everything today causes cancer … One day someone will determine smoking is actually beneficial … I could walk out tomorrow and get hit by a car, so why not enjoy life?"

What crap! I was so wrapped up in my denial that I searched for evidence to prove that smoking could actually be beneficial. I had to find a rationale for my erratic behavior.

The years went by and so did my college dreams. I did not get into an American medical school, so I went to Germany to study medicine. But instead, I fell in love with a Turkish woman who wanted to come to the States. I moved back home. Over ten years had passed since my freshman year in college. Somehow, ten years later, I was more than eighty pounds overweight—nearly 240 pounds—and now smoking close to three packs of cigarettes a day. What was happening to me?

CHAPTER 4

Soul Searching

When I was young, I promised myself that I would always stay open-minded and youthful. I would never let my age cause me to become negative and closed-minded. In my twenties, I was in tiptop shape—no worries, free-spirited, exciting to be with, and extremely spiritual. After college, I was thirty-two years old, out of shape, without a girlfriend, and in a job I hated, and I did not like the person I had become. What had happened to the Joey that I knew and loved when I was younger? Where had he gone? Not only was I out of shape physically, but also my inner spirit was stripped. I felt empty inside, and I wanted to change everything in my life, but I did not know how.

Fear and self-hate had crept into my consciousness. I felt out of control and knew I had to do something to get my life back together. I did not like the person I had become, and I wanted badly to quit smoking, but it just was not happening. I hated the cigarette smell that clung to my clothes and lingered throughout my house. I hated the hold smoking had on me. I did not like being controlled by a substance, and knew I had to make a choice. I would not let another ten years go by, only to find out that I was not happy with the path I had chosen. I knew that my life was falling apart, but I did not want to examine who I was.

I decided to go to an ashram (a spiritual retreat) in upstate New York and participate in a silence for three days. That period of silence helped me focus; it was necessary to discipline myself and quiet my mind in order to focus inwardly. Shortly after, I made three important decisions: I had to quit smoking; I had to quit my job; and I had to regain my youth and find happiness again.

I was burned out from my job, and I'd worked without taking a vacation for two years. I was now smoking three packs a day and needed a long vacation to rethink my life. Smoking was destroying me. I could not breathe at night. I was always tired, nervous, and irritable. When I looked in the mirror, I did not like who I saw. I always believed that everyone has a part in this world. A fat, depressed, nervous, irritable man was not the role I wanted to play in the game of life. I truly hated cigarettes, but I also loved how they seemed to relieve stress temporarily. I wondered how I could possibly quit when everything in my life was falling apart. All I knew was that I had to stop!

Smoking was destroying my nerves and robbing me of my youth. I knew that it was destroying my circulation. My hands and feet were constantly cold, and I couldn't jog or ride a bike because I was always short of breath. I then decided to make a quit date. I would quit smoking when I went on vacation. I knew this was another procrastination plot, but it was the best that I could do. I made a decision to make a change, not only with quitting smoking, but also with changing my life for the better. This was my first true decision: I knew that after my vacation, I wasn't coming home a smoker. I wasn't going to allow myself to smoke anymore. It was the first time that I got angry at my inaction to quit! I was also angry with the tobacco companies and upset with smoking, tobacco, and nicotine in general. I knew I was stronger than my addiction, and I was going to prove it! From that moment on, I knew some of my strength was back. The old spiritual Joey was coming back.

Toward the end of this book, you will also have to make the decision to never smoke again. You must also find it within yourself to give up your fear of quitting, and instead believe in yourself. You must also start to question your beliefs and actions about why you smoke and accept the truth about smoking, your addiction to nicotine, and how the four thousand chemicals in tobacco cause an adverse affect on your health and the health of others that you smoke around. Smoking is finally becoming taboo in society. All across the United States, states and cities are going smoke-free, making it illegal to smoke in any public place. It is estimated that more than 1,100 deaths occur in the United States every day due to smoking-related illnesses, about 350 each day in the United Kingdom. In Ireland about 6,700 deaths a year are caused by tobacco smoke. Cigarette smoking kills! There is nothing nice to say about smoking. It sucks.

The day that you make the choice to quit smoking and never put another cigarette in your mouth will change your life forever, and you will be a nonsmoker. You will be instructed later on how to quit cold turkey and throw those cigarettes away, once and for all. So enjoy your addiction, for now. Smoke on! But realize that the time will come when you will have to choose the correct path and quit smoking. So please get ready to give up your habit. Start accepting that you have the power, the will, and the control to be a nonsmoker.

Smoking has no advantages. You also need to commit yourself to being a nonsmoker for the rest of your life. This shall be the seventh rule between us. Now, please don't freak out about quitting. You're still in the early part of this book, and I won't ask you to think about quitting until the very end. However, if you choose to quit in the middle of this book, so be it—great!

CHAPTER 5
Finding Myself Again

I needed a vacation to be alone; I needed to rethink my life and escape the fast track of New York City. Not knowing where to go, I searched the Internet for hours to find that special place. I cruised Web sites of various spiritual resorts, meditation camps, yoga retreats, fasting camps, fat farms, quit-smoking camps, and typical vacation spots around the continent. Then I came across a Web page with a photo of the Dalai Lama. Right then, I knew I had to search no longer. Nepal and Tibet were the places that I would travel to. I was excited about going. Then I remembered that I had made a promise to quit smoking on my next vacation. That meant I could not come back home a smoker.

I started to get anxious about quitting and began rationalizing that quitting while on vacation would not be wise, since I would be miserable. But this time I was adamant, and knew I could no longer postpone quitting, so I kept my promise and agreed to quit in Nepal.

I knew this vacation would wipe out my savings, but I also knew I had no choice. The next day I wrote a letter to my supervisor, stating that I was taking a month off from work. She did not offer much resistance, because everyone knew I was suffering from job burnout. My boss knew that if my request was not granted, I would quit on the spot; she said yes.

I booked a flight and packed my bags and was soon on my way to the Himalayas. The flight took more than a day, but it was pleasant to be alone and in silence. I spent the whole flight without speaking (or smoking).

CHAPTER 6

Arriving in Nepal

Almost thirty-six hours later, I was finally in Nepal, and my first reaction when I went outside the airport was to have a cigarette. I must have smoked three of them, one right after the other, as I waited for a cab to drive me to my Himalayan meditation resort. My craving was back. I thought about how difficult quitting was going to be.

The taxi arrived and I was on my way, some ninety miles still to go. The ride was at times depressing and shocking. Everywhere I looked, I saw poverty and filth like I have never seen in my life. I saw families living in cardboard boxes, along with their dogs, chickens, and cows. Children played in the street; their only toys were the rocks along the road. The air was thick and polluted, so bad I could not breathe. The noise of the city was unbearable and constant, with traffic and horns honking every second.

At first I wondered what on earth I was doing in this country, and then I thought, There is no way I can quit smoking here. As I looked out the window, I noticed that a lot of people were smoking. I grew more anxious and wanted to get out to the countryside where the air would be clean and hopefully, less polluted.

I continued to smoke one cigarette after another. I was now hacking away from the air pollutants, the heat of the city, the cigarette smoke from the cab driver, and my own smoking. I continued to cough non-stop. The driver, who was named Pradip, gave me an herbal throat lozenge. He told me he coughed all the time and that sometimes he coughed up blood. Immediately I thought of tuberculosis or some infectious disease, but then he said that he had lung cancer. He told me how smoking relieved the tensions he felt inside. I was at a loss for words. I thought this guy was in denial or wanted a good tip. I said I was sorry, and I wanted to give him a lecture about smoking—but how could I, when I smoked more than two packs a day? I was traveling down the same path as him. In twenty years, I would probably also be a victim to smoking-related lung cancer.

While traveling, I began to notice the billboard advertisements throughout the city. There were billboards and neon signs everywhere I looked. The western influence was blatant in Nepal. I noticed cigarette and beer advertisements plastered on buildings, billboards, and windows everywhere. This is what the Nepalese had learned about Americans—how to smoke and drink alcohol. How was it possible that these people could afford to pay for cigarettes and alcohol, when they could barely support life's bare necessities?

The tobacco industry has found new avenues to promote their products—the young and the poor. In the streets, it seemed every fifth person had a cancer stick in their mouth. It was sad to see so many smoking, especially the young. I was disgusted to see so many Nepalese addicted to smoking. Those who did not have enough money for food bought cigarettes. This brought me back to my first experience with smoking, how cool I had felt when I smoked my first cigarette. In Nepal, I noticed some of the same advertisements that I had seen growing up as a child—the strong cowboy with a cigarette in his mouth rounding up cows, and the funny-looking camel. It was strange to see even a pregnant woman smoking as she walked along the road. I told the cabby to look at her, and I said, "Doesn't she know how dangerous smoking is to her unborn child?"

I did not like what I was seeing in Nepal. I was upset at the tobacco industry for using these innocent people to sell a product. I now began to see the tobacco industry as legal drug dealers. It is one of the most addictive substances known to man, with the ability to cause death, yet so loosely regulated. It was evident by all the billboards in Nepal that the focus was on children and women.

According to reports from the American Cancer Society, the World Health Organization, and the International Union Against Cancer, tobacco-related cancer is increasing in developing countries. Currently about half of the world's tobacco-related cancer deaths occur in developing countries, and that's expected to increase to more than 70 percent by 2020.

I told Pradip that I was through being a slave to tobacco. Cigarettes have destroyed so many lives, including his. We talked about how we were addicted to nicotine, and how many times we had both tried to quit, but failed. We laughed about our addiction to hide how out-of-control we felt inside. Pradip finally admitted that he was sick of smoking and admitted that it would cost him his life. He asked himself why he was so stupid. He described how guilty he felt, being married with children and how afraid he was of dying, and leaving his wife alone to care for the children. I asked him if he had received radiation for the tumors. He did not know what I was talking about. He was under no treatment for his cancer.

Pradip probably won't live another five years. I often had to hold back my tears as he talked about dying. This was a huge reality check for me. Wow, after hearing his story, how could I continue being a smoker? I was not into giving myself cancer. It's different if you develop cancer because of heredity, but to contract lung cancer from smoking was something that I did not want to happen to me. Even as I was thinking about quitting, I went into my pocket and lit another cigarette. We had been sharing ideas for almost two hours now, and I felt as if I knew him. Continuing to smoke would be idiotic. This was my signal and the strength that I needed to end my habit forever. I finished my cigarette, and Pradip now began to light up another cigarette.

I told Pradip, "Let's do it together. Let's quit for your health and also for my health. I want to live and I want you to live, to be able to see your children grow up. I am quitting for you, my friend."

Pradip looked at me as if I was crazy, and he did not believe me, but then he looked again into my eyes and realized I was serious. We were communicating without words. I felt sad and full of rage as I also saw his own rage and his pain in his eyes. He opened his pack of cigarettes and spit on them twice. He closed his pack and uttered something under his breath in Nepalese. Then he crushed the pack in his hands and threw it out the window. I did the same, uttering "Never again will I be a victim." I felt good and knew that after this symbolic gesture, I would never again go back to smoking.

This is when I developed my strong hatred towards tobacco. I was tired of being used. I did not like being dominated by a product, especially from a company that had absolutely no respect for its consumers, a company that had been accused in the past of lying, stealing, and cheating their customers. How could I respect an organization that targets products to the poor, the uneducated, the young, and the innocent?

The cab ride was over. Pradip helped me get my bags to the gate, and we hugged each other and said goodbye. I had finally arrived at my destination, a Tibetan ashram located on top of a mountain within the most beautiful forest that I could imagine. This was the birthplace of Buddha. I could not believe how beautiful this place was. There were waterfalls, a breathtaking mountain range, yaks, cows, goats, monkeys, and sheep. I felt like Adam in the Garden of Eden. My cabin was a huge hut straight out of some Tarzan movie.

Everywhere I looked was a new adventure. One thing that was difficult for me to adjust to was all the insects and other creatures in my hut. There were no windows to protect me from the jungle environment outside. Anything that wanted to come into my hut could simply enter through the window, which was covered only by draperies. I noticed three lizards on the ceiling of my hut. I had been told beforehand about the lizards. I knew they were a blessing, as they were responsible for eating the insects within the hut. I witnessed one of these lizards catching a huge flying water bug. I accepted this and greeted my new pets. Just after 9:59, the light went out. I now had no electricity. I freaked. I was in total blackness. I proceeded to the office where I was told that lights go out at 10 p.m. I was a person who normally retired at 3 a.m. I had to get used to retiring early.

The second night at the ashram, a visitor was waiting for me when I opened the hut's door. An Indian cobra was laying on the ground, mere inches from the front door. I have never been so frightened in my entire life; my heart was pounding and racing. I was terrified! I just stood there in total shock, and within a minute; the snake slithered away. No more than an hour later, as I was walking up the mountain for a meditation class, I almost stepped on another snake. It stood up and went to bite me, but I ran seconds before the strike; I guess it wasn't my time to go. It looked like a viper of some sort. Halfway to the administration office, I met the groundskeeper and told him about my incidents with the snakes. He replied that there was no reason to be worried or afraid, since the forest was filled with animals. It was unlikely that they would bite me. He told me that the snakes were well fed and they wouldn't bite without a reason. His assurance was enough for me to decide to leave this paradise and do some traveling in the city.

I could handle the garden snakes that I had often seen in Bayside, New York, where I was raised. I was, however, unable to handle a wilderness filled with cobras, vipers, boas, and pythons that were indigenous to Nepal. Not only was this forest filled with snakes, there were also big, giant roaches that flew and made strange noises. I left that afternoon and continued my journey out of Eden.

I was getting a bit agitated, as I had not had a cigarette for almost three days. I began to complain and whine about everything. I was irritable and pessimistic, and absolutely nothing went right. I wanted to start smoking again, but I held strong, and I told my whining mind to "shut up." I was tired of listening to my thoughts complaining about everything. It was difficult for me to shut my mind off so, instead, I watched my emotions flare up without analyzing or judging them. I let them roam by as the clouds floated along the sky. I learned this technique in one of the meditation classes that I took in the mountains. I knew that I was here in Nepal for a reason.

Refocusing my thought patterns, I stopped complaining and began to look at all the beauty that surrounded me. I was less than four days away from Tibet. What on earth did I have to complain about? Many people dream of traveling to Nepal and Tibet, and all I could think about was a damn cigarette. How crazy was that? The awesome mountains and the blue skies weren't enough to soothe my active mind. The urge for a cigarette was driving me mad. Once I took control of my thoughts, I began to notice the splendor again. I noticed that the urge only lasted about three minutes. After every urge to smoke, I took slow, rhythmic breaths in, to the count of eight, then held my breath to a count of four, than exhaled to a count of fourteen. I'd read somewhere on the Internet that rhythmic, controlled breathing helps with the cravings of smoking when quitting. It seemed to work.

My next stop was Pokhara to do some trekking. I was looking forward to hiking the Royal Trek, the same route that Prince Charles had trekked that made that path notable. It was a four-day hike with some excellent views of the Anapurna and Manaslu mountain ranges. The trek in itself was not demanding; the altitude was about 1,500 meters, and there were basically no steep inclines. However, as a result of being a smoker, I could not complete it. I fainted from exhaustion and had to be driven back into town after the second day. I felt totally like a loser. I was pissed and disappointed in myself—especially noticing that a couple, who seemed to be in their sixties had passed me during my trek.

Unable to do any trekking worth my while, I decided to hit the road and start traveling toward Tibet via public transportation. Most of the tourists I met told me to take the private bus used by Americans and Europeans, but I had to get a visa. I thought, Why would I want to do that? I am an American and I lived in Europe for two years, so why would I go to Nepal to hang out with Americans and Europeans? I was here to experience the culture, so I took the public bus instead. After three hours, I realized why I was told to take the private buses. The public bus had no air conditioning and it reeked of caustic gas fumes. The bus made many stops. The journey was long, grueling, and often totally unbearable. I must have experienced every emotion known to man. I was sick of this country and I wanted to go back home to luxury. I was getting severe headaches now from the cigarette withdrawal and I felt sick. At times, I doubted my decision to rough it out by taking the public bus and wanted to go back to Katmandu. Traveling the mountain range of the Himalayas was an experience I would never forget.

The trip had many ups and downs. The first bad experience was during one of our pit stops when we discovered that one bus had not made the journey to Tibet two nights ago and had fallen off the cliff. All within the bus were pronounced dead. I felt sick and was now terrified. I did not want to go back on the bus. Every bone in my body was shaking. I needed something to calm my nerves. I raised my hands to ask, "God, why me?" I then went to the country store and bought a pack of cigarettes. I was a nervous wreck, sweating from the heat, and my headache was now a migraine. I hadn't smoked in four days.

I thought that my withdrawal symptoms would go away after four days, but they just got stronger. I hated everyone in sight, and I was in a constant, bad mood. The bus driver drove like a maniac, and I just knew we were all going to die. I thought that I was cursed, since I was traveling to Tibet via an illegal route and believed it to be my destiny. The snakes had attempted to take my life at the ashram, and now I believed I would die on this bus. I was now paranoid. I could see the newspaper headlines in my head: American Man Dies on Route to Tibet in an Unauthorized Travel Bus.

I told myself I was done with trying to quit smoking. I just wanted a cigarette to feel myself again, so I could cope and stop the pain. Just as I started to open the pack, the bus driver called us to get onboard. I was saved for the moment, and my willpower came back. I realized that all of these emotions I felt were from my addiction. I told myself the addiction and the craziness wouldn't last forever. I kept saying to myself: I am stronger than my thoughts. I didn't really believe it at the time, but I knew from Psychology 101 that you are your thoughts. If only I could convince my psyche to believe that I no longer needed cigarettes and that I actually loathed them.

Then I remembered the pain/pleasure principle from college that describes how we, as humans, tend to seek pleasure and avoid pain—and everything is focused around this concept. One way was to exchange a drug-using habit, such as smoking, for other pleasurable, drug-free activities. So, in order to quit smoking and remain a nonsmoker for the rest of my life, I needed to stop focusing on the how painful quitting smoking was, and instead substitute my cravings with something pleasurable, such as jogging, trekking, meditating, praying, breathing techniques, etc. I also needed to view the act of smoking as a negative, so I would not want to smoke again.

I knew that smoking was not the answer to calming my nerves. I had good reasons to be nervous, but I also knew that I was in control of my nerves. Suddenly, Pradip entered my mind and I remembered the promise we had made together to never smoke again. I also associated smoking with lung cancer and had seen the blood in Pradip's phlegm every time he coughed up phlegm. This was not a pleasant sight and was enough to convince my psyche to believe that starting smoking again was the negative—the pain—while remaining a nonsmoker was the pleasure. I was a man of my word, and I was determined not to break the promise I had made to Pradip and to myself, even if Pradip's story about him having cancer was only told for me to feel sorry and to give him a good tip.

The bus was stopping again for food. I would hold strong and not smoke. To make sure of this, I opened the pack of cigarettes that I bought at the last pit stop, spit in them as Pradip did in the cab, and crushed them with my foot and said to myself: Never again. I choose health over disease. I felt proud of myself while also feeling ashamed for almost giving in to the addiction. I was still in a bad mood and still had a headache, so when I got back on the bus I went to sleep.

I must have slept for more than six hours when I was awakened by a guy named Ludan, who wanted me to look out my window to watch the sunrise. I was not in a good mood, being that my migraine had not let up. I was upset that Ludan kept on chatting and touching my leg to get me up. I thought that these people touch way too much. What the heck is he touching my leg for? I looked out the window and saw nothing—there was no sunrise, only gray clouds and mountains. I thought he was crazy. I closed my eyes again, and in less than fifteen minutes, Ludan tapped me again, but this time on my shoulder. I wanted to yell at him, but I kept my cool and realized that I wasn't in New York. So I woke up and chatted with Ludan. About ten minutes later, the sun rose from behind the mountains.

I felt as if I was dreaming. It was absolutely the most awesome thing I had ever seen in my life. Mountains were all around me, and the sky was filled with many different hues of blues, reds, golden-oranges, yellows, and greens. Seeing the painted sky through the mountains at sunrise was what I would expect to see in heaven. Witnessing such beauty bestowed upon me a new sense of spirituality. I would not have believed such a sunset could exist without being digitally enhanced, and had never suspected nature could be this wonderful. Nepal was simply heavenly, and I would have paid the price of my trip just to witness such a sunrise. The bus stopped so that we could get a better view. I could see the tip of Mount Everest and the surrounding mountains. I felt really blessed to be here. This was nature at its grandest, truly meditative. Some saluted the sun with a yogi dance. Others sat and meditated. I too sat and began meditating, and somehow everything seemed just right. I don't know what it did to me, but I just felt better. My migraine was gone, and my fear started to subside. It was kind of strange, but I felt like a new man. I felt reborn.

CHAPTER 7
Our Existence on Earth

As a scientist, I was trained to believe that the world was created by some random accident—the big bang theory of evolution ... that we are all here on this earth merely by chance, that as humans, we have evolved through an explosion from the cosmos, as a result of which simple amino acids were created within the ocean, which begat primitive organisms, which evolved into higher organisms, eventually mutating to other plants and animals, leading to the evolution of humans. Evolution states the progression of humans through changes occurring over billions of years.

If that is supposed to be true, then why don't we have any fossil records of the intermediate species of evolution? How did we come from the ocean and become land animals? Was there a half-lizard/half-ape intermediate fossil found that I don't know about?

We are all free to believe what we want, and this is what makes us special and different. Some believe the theory of creation is just as unbelievable. The only problem I have with the big bang theory is that if it was true, then life was a random, non-conscious event? However, believing it keeps you from realizing what is important and essential to life, which is that nature is too perfect and ordered to have been created without instruction. Your birth is no accident, and neither is mine. The existence of every man, woman, and every living organism is not by chance. Your life is a miracle, and we all have a purpose in life.

Somehow, we have forgotten that life is important. Not just human life, but all life. Accepting this and allowing it to enter your perception is extremely difficult for most people ... because when you accept that life is important, you have no other choice but to respect yourself and every living thing in this universe. The choice to allow yourself to be controlled by a habit, especially one as destructive as smoking, can only mean that you have no regard for your life or your health. You simply cannot want good health, yet choose to smoke; it's a paradox. The trip to Nepal gave me the chance to discover that missing link to my soul. Nepal taught me how to go inside myself and find my spirituality again. It also opened my eyes to the world around me.

Our world has fallen apart because we have forgotten that everything on earth is interconnected. We are all part of another. This is what I hope you will gain from reading this book—increased awareness. You are important and so is your health. Smoking—and believing that it won't affect your health—is foolish. In Nepal, I experienced every emotion known to man, even emotions of which I was ashamed of—pain, hate, fear, prejudice, and many others. These emotions helped me focus on my inner self. This is what this book is all about: relearning, rediscovering, and dealing with your spirituality and common truth.

Please don't let the word "spirituality" turn you off. One of my fears as I wrote this book was that I might offend some or turn others off. Just try to stay focused and keep an open mind, without negatively judging the words in this book. This will help you gain new insights into yourself and within your world, and ultimately will help you quit smoking forever.

Quitting smoking is more complicated than just wanting to quit. You must also change your thought processes associated with smoking and the world as you have been seeing it.

We as a nation have become too smart for our own good. We tend to overanalyze everything. We also tend to judge others by their physical appearance or material possessions, instead of what is inside. The new millennium culture has become brainwashed by only what is logical. Thinking outside of the box is not popular. My spirituality was stripped by the scientific doctrines, theories, and laws that were taught to me in college. We are becoming a nation of "if you can't touch it, feel it, or see it, then it does not exist." This is extremely gullible, incorrect, arrogant, and ignorant. We as humans are only as good as the instruments that we possess. You really can't prove anything in this world. You can only attempt to disprove it.

For example, before man invented the light microscope, bacteria did not exist because they were too small to see with the naked eye. We could not see them or feel them, but they had the ability to kill us before we discovered them. You don't have to see something to believe in its power. The electron microscope allowed us, under high magnification, to see tiny organisms and gave us a new insight into the invisible universe. Viruses and bacteria have always existed—but before the invention of the microscope, if you had told anyone that you believed there were invisible bugs within your body, which caused your nose to run and gave your body terrible pain, you would have been considered insane. Remember that we don't always have the tools to know what is real or what is untrue, so just keep your mind open.

The soul is the instrument that gives us a better understanding of spirit and the workings of the universe. It is how we discover there is a higher spirit, called God. Without going inward to find your inner soul, it is impossible to realize that God exists. Today, if you speak about religion in the simplest terms, you are perceived as a fanatic or a believer in fairy tales. God is becoming nothing more than a fictitious character in the Bible. Why is it so cool today not to believe in God? Science and the belief in religion can coexist, and they do. One of the smartest men of all time, Albert Einstein, has been quoted as saying, "Science without religion is lame; religion without science is blind." Going to Nepal and Tibet was no accident. It was necessary for me to regain my spirituality and to write this book for those who want to quit. Being in Nepal gave me the opportunity to be surrounded by positive, spiritual people who believe in a higher calling and a reason for life.

My message here is to reopen yourself to others and to a higher calling. This book is your first step. Stay young and keep your mind receptive to new ideas and thoughts. I noticed in Nepal that I was the instrument to my feelings. I controlled them and my emotions. There were times when I arrived in Nepal that all I could focus on was the dirt, the poverty, the beggars, and the smell from the rickshaws. Then when I allowed myself not to focus on what was wrong with Nepal, I began to notice the Himalayas, Mount Everest, the amazing sunsets, the yaks, the Nepalese culture, and all the wonderful things the country had to offer. I could have focused on all the negative things, and I would have come back home with a horrible experience. But instead, I changed my mindset to the positive, and Nepal became the most wonderful experience of my life.

It is the same with quitting smoking. You can focus on withdrawal symptoms and gaining weight, or you can focus on the health benefits and the ability to take control of your life. If you focus on how much better your life will be without cigarettes, quitting smoking will be easier. When you quit smoking, you will have more money in your pocket. You will no longer ruin your clothes and furniture from dropped ashes, and you won't have to dry clean your fine clothing as much from the horrible smell of cigarette smoke. The brain is an extremely powerful and limitless organ, but without being connected to the spirit, it is virtually nonfunctional. If you fill your brain with negative thoughts, your output will be negative and self-destructive. If you feed it understanding, acceptance, and love, your output in life will be harmony, comfort, happiness, and life.

CHAPTER 8

The Message

Going to Nepal revealed to me that no matter where I traveled, my conditions in life would remain the same unless I changed my way of thinking. Before going to Nepal, I thought of my life as empty and I was somewhat depressed. I could not pinpoint why I felt that way, I just felt so blah. During meditation, I began to question what was going on in my life that made me so unhappy. While meditating, I learned how to erase my negative thoughts and focus on the more constructive things. Calming was merely accepting the feelings and caring about them without judging or regretting the past.

This book is a spiritual guide to get you back on your way to truth and understanding. You must realize that you are in control of your success. You also need to understand that no matter how convincing my words are, if you choose to ignore them or shut yourself out without finding out why you do the things you do, then you won't gain much from this book or any quit-smoking book on the market. The message here is to go inward.

You've tried to quit smoking but failed? In order for you to combat your addiction, you will have to remember the past mistakes that led you to start again after you had quit. Realizing your mistakes and why you went back to smoking will be the key for you to never make the same mistake again. It will be your secret to remaining a nonsmoker for the rest of your life. Learn how to channel your energy on the positive rather than the negative. Don't focus on how difficult it is going to be to quit. Instead, focus on how you will do it this time! You *can* quit smoking and *you will quit smoking* if you learn how to take one step at a time. The important thing is to stay focused on the present, the here and now, while reading this book. Not the past, nor the future.

We as humans tend to focus on all the things we have not accomplished, and we forget those we have. Before Nepal, I worried about my future. I worried about my past. I worried about quitting smoking. I worried about my weight. I worried so much that it was difficult for me to sleep at night. My mind was racing, and I did not know how to shut it off. I realized that all this worrying was the main reason I remained stagnant. I never produced energy to make my dreams a reality. I knew that from this day onward, I had to take control of my life.

If you want success, you must create it first in your mind, and then you must make it happen. I knew that misfortunes, pain, and suffering would continue to revisit my life and that I would have no control over this. No one is immune to such things. However, I did have control over my thoughts. I was responsible for smoking, and I was responsible for gaining weight when I quit.

I remember a Tibetan saying to me as I whined about how small the dinner portions were in this one particular restaurant, that one should not eat to feel satisfied—but instead, one should eat to nourish the body. That simple statement made me realize that my body is a temple. I reached a new comfort zone and learned that I was in control of my destiny. I also learned that our reality is how we deal with difficult moments. You, for example, may be unhappy with your job, your boss, and the way your life turned out, but if you learn from what is difficult, you will gain life experience, which can help you cope when you really need it. Learning to deal with a difficult and demanding coworker who is driving you crazy is one way to learn patience and how to deal with difficult people. Visualize all experiences as lessons in life. Instead of being a victim, become a student of life and its powerful lessons.

The world looks quite different if you get away from the battlefield and stop taking it so seriously. Learn to overcome your obstacles and start living. Getting out of New York for more than a month gave me the opportunity to talk and share ideas with the Nepalese and Buddhists. I witnessed poverty that I could never imagine. All the miseries of humanity were in front of my face for me to witness, yet I met some of the most spiritual people in my life. Some were very poor, but they were nonetheless content with their existence. There was less drama in their lives.

In Nepal, I discovered simplicity and started to notice the positive instead of the negative. Just being born in America is a blessing, as we have so many opportunities, unlike Nepal, where it seems impossible for some to achieve their dreams because of the caste system. What I admired the most about the Nepalese and the Tibetans were their honesty and their innate understanding of mankind and the workings of the universe. The most valuable lesson that I learned traveling to a developing country was compassion and wisdom. Having compassion for others less fortunate gave me a new sense of compassion for myself. By having compassion for myself, I quit hurting myself and realized that my smoking addiction was a destructive behavior that I would no longer allow. It was after my journey that I discovered that what I wanted to do was help others quit smoking—and thus this book.

Getting in touch with people who want to quit smoking, or those who are bothered by secondhand smoke reminds me of my history and my own suffering with tobacco, nicotine, and the addiction. I turned my love of smoking to a hatred of smoking, and have used that energy to help others quit by giving seminars on quitting smoking. Before leaving for Nepal, a close friend told me I was not happy unless drama was going on in my life. I felt empty inside. I had experienced so many disappointments that I was searching for answers and occasionally questioning my existence. From my journey I realized that disappointment, mishaps, disabilities, addictions, failing, death, loneliness, and separation are normal and part of living. Everyone has experienced degrees of unhappiness in their life. Pain and hardship are not personal and are not "the wrath of God." Experiences, both pleasurable and painful, are necessary in order for an individual to grow and learn.

My problem was that I ran from my failures or denied them. I was a great procrastinator. It took being alone with myself in silence to realize this all. We all need a pause in life, to recapture and confront our beliefs. In the silence of your privacy you discover what is and what is not, and you open your soul and heart to your reality within. I will teach you very basic and simple relaxation techniques to help you challenge yourself. If you run from what is difficult, then you will never learn how to correct the problem and experience it again. Pain is an inevitable part of life. The "Why me?" syndrome, wishing that pain, misfortune, and failure did not exist in your life, means you wish, hope, even expect the universe to treat you differently than every living being on this planet. But suffering, death, and pain are normal in our lives.

Of course getting over an addiction is tough. If it wasn't, there wouldn't be a need for this book. Although more than about 25 percent of American adults continue to smoke, about 70 percent of them want to quit. Withdrawal is a difficult process. When I quit, years later I still had cravings for nicotine, and about 20 percent of ex-smokers still have occasional cravings for cigarettes. Developing hatred toward smoking ensured that I would never again succumb to my cravings for nicotine. I also know that once you are addicted to a substance, you are *always* addicted to that substance. So I knew that I could never smoke any tobacco product again. Any attempts to quit are never a waste of time, since the amount of smoking is reduced during these periods. Please, never think that quitting is a waste of your time or effort. Life is not perfect. We fail and we try again. The key here is to learn from your mistakes, so you don't repeat them.

Dealing with issues that come your way from time to time is just the way life happens. No one is exempt from misfortune. Just before submitting the first edition of this book, I went dancing and broke my leg in three places, had surgery, and was confined to a wheelchair for almost three months, but I looked at the positive side of the accident. I had more time to write the book. Why me?

Why not me? Stuff happens. Realizing that addiction is difficult to combat, and knowing there will be many obstacles to come in your path to make you want to smoke again, is normal.

I want to liberate you from the slavery of tobacco and nicotine by means of transforming your perception of what smoking is and what it isn't. This transformation is a way of thinking outside of the box and looking at your experiences in life—the good with the bad—and realizing that it is okay. Your addiction in many ways is selfish because you are jeopardizing your health, and this affects others. You will learn that you have the power to quit.

CHAPTER 9

Lessons of Simplicity

1. Belief in God and prayer is rational and okay.
2. Learn from the negative so you don't have to relive it.
3. Remember that pain and hardship are experienced by all. Nothing is personal.
4. Focus on the positive.
5. Create you own destiny.
6. Realize that you are in control of your thoughts.
7. Don't judge yourself or others.
8. Live life.
9. Be honest to yourself.
10. Be strong and courageous.
11. Mellow out; don't take the world and people so seriously.
12. Trust life.
13. Be open-minded.
14. Be nice.
15. Listen when people speak.

16. Be aware of the moment.

17. Be aware of what you speak.

18. Be mindful of your thoughts.

19. Take pride and worth in your self.

20. Know that you have all the power that you need.

We are all teachers of our own unique journey, and we all hold a piece of the puzzle. Stay open, share, learn, and listen.

These are just a few of the messages I learned in the Himalayas. It is not life's mistakes and adversities that matter. But instead, it is what we do to correct the misfortunes that tend to pop up from time to time.

To quit smoking, you need to recognize some of the tough hard facts that sometimes will sound a bit strong, but there are no in-betweens. Smoking has the power to kill you. You are paying the tobacco companies your hard-earned money to cause you harm. Yes, it may be true that you may not die from cancer. You could instead get a heart attack or even a stroke. No one is forcing you to smoke. So why are you gambling with your health? I don't want to scare you. I want you only to realize what you are doing to yourself. Denial plays a big role in a smoker's life and it helps keep the smoker attached to tobacco products.

The "I can quit anytime that I want to" or the "I'm just not ready to quit now" excuses are your mind taking control! You must admit your addiction and try to conquer it, instead of denying that smoking controls you and your thoughts. I know this since I have been in denial for each of my seven attempts at quitting. This book is structured so you can also go inside yourself and build strength in order to "Nic Your Habit."

CHAPTER 10

Non-Judgment

The Himalayas also taught me a couple of important lessons—nonjudgment and silence of the mind. It was only when I was silent that I was able to see the world in a different life. I noticed how blue the sky was, I noticed the many different varieties of plants and trees, my sense of smell increased, and in fact all of my senses were heightened. It was within my silence and the ability to shut my mind off, and also the ability to catch myself being critical and judging, that I opened myself to a new world where I did not focus on the negative, but began to notice and focus on the positives. Witnessing everything around you and being aware of your environment, your thoughts, your fears, and your wants, but learning how to not judge them, is a true gift to open your soul.

Open your eyes and stay focused. Become aware of your actions: why you smoke, when you smoke, how it makes you feel. We do so many things unconsciously and this is how the addiction prevails. The world is beautiful depending upon what you focus on. If you focus on the eleven o'clock news and listen to all the crime statistics, you will see the world as a mess. If you focus on the beauty of life and the good of man, you will start to see the world as miraculous. Instead of judging yourself and others, start focusing on the present, instead of worrying about what you don't have, and what others have that you want. You also must learn to stop trying to analyze your past, as if it was totally responsible for your present or future.

You are the only one responsible for your present and your future. If you live in the past or in the future, you will tend to neglect the "here and now." Your present is what makes your future, and it also helps you conquer past mistakes. Nonjudgment of yourself and others is crucial to self-improvement. Why on earth would you worry about what someone else is doing with his or her life, when there is so much you need to do with yours? This is one of the most important lessons in life. Fix yourself; stop trying to fix your friends, spouse, family, or neighbors. This book is about fixing your nicotine addiction. This must be your main concern. Focusing on quitting yourself. You don't need to quit with your partner; you are both different people. Focus first on what you need to do, so you are better able to help the ones you love. Remember, the teacher comes when the student is ready, and most people learn best by example. Quitting smoking will be the most important thing that you can do for yourself and those you love. Quitting smoking may just save your life!

Our perception of life is based on our own experiences. No two experiences are the same, therefore it is impossible to judge others or know what is best for them, since you have not experienced their world. Your experiences are usually just perfect for you and what you need to learn in this lifetime.

Imagine how easy life would be if we just focused on our own business. The world seems to give each one of us special and individual lessons that help us mature and grow. Some lessons are truly meant to teach, while others are just random acts of nature.

Each person has a different history and path which makes them unique. These past experiences affect how one views the world. Our past is an integral part of who we are and who we *think* we are in the present. What I am saying is that your past may give you a foundation to build upon, but it never has to limit you. We can't hide from the past, nor should we live in it. Many of us blame our parents for being who we are today. You are not the way you are because of past events, since they do not decide who you are or how you think. You make that decision. The past can only affect your future if you allow it to continue to hold you in its grip. Please, don't get me wrong. I am not being insensitive to your past, nor do I want you to deny your past. Instead, I want you to take hold of your life so you can overcome what has held you back from being all that you want to be.

Your misfortune in this world does not predict your future. You control your own destiny by learning from past events and by making good choices in the present. Life gives us many chances and opportunities to overcome our obstacles. We must, however, open the door. Some of you keep your doors closed because you are afraid. Others are closed because of rebellion, while some remain closed to opportunity purely out of ignorance.

Escaping a past problem or situation can be extremely difficult. However, overcoming a past failure brings a gamut of rewards. Combating your smoking habit will lead you to many more triumphs. If you choose to learn from your past, instead of living from the events of your past, you will experience growth. If you do not learn from it, you will repeat it, and this will become a vicious cycle your children will inherit.

We all have mishaps and we all have addictive behaviors. We also feel sad or lonely at different times. We all have lost or will lose people that we love. Some lose loved ones to old age, others lose loved ones to horrible crimes or illnesses. Nonjudgment has helped me accept my mistakes, my wrong choices, my mishaps and disabilities, and those disabilities of others. Choose to live in the present and work on fixing the past so that you can grow and gain your rewards in the future. Realizing that nothing is personal has helped me get on with my life, control my own destiny, and choose the path I always wanted

CHAPTER 11

Fear and Courage

There is no one on earth who has not felt deprived or has not made mistakes. We have all been dealt a bad hand at one time or another. Some start off with many advantages, others with less. Some use their advantages, others simply pass them by. Opportunity is always available and within reach. Fear is the only thing that limits us. It is your fear that keeps you bound to your cigarette addiction. The fear of losing the battle, after so many attempts, is the reason you procrastinate. Give yourself some good advice and "Nic Your Habit." One of my best friends, Chloe, once said to me, "If you never push yourself to go beyond, especially the things in your life that are difficult, then you will never truly advance yourself." Chloe had a fear of flying, so she enrolled herself in flying lessons. She now has her pilot's license and is thinking about buying a plane. She realized that she was in control of her fears. Your fears should never control your life.

Fear will kill you faster than any illness known to man. Fear destroys our relationships with others, yourself, and the Almighty. Fear is an emotion that stems from your past experiences or misconceptions. The way to erase fear is to combat it. This is why I stress being honest with yourself as being so important. Some people are so dishonest with their feelings that they find it difficult to be true to themselves. Time alone, even with five-minute relaxation techniques, will help you uncover some of these fears. Have the courage to keep on trying. You are reading this book, and if you have taken it seriously so far, I congratulate you! When you realize that smoking does absolutely nothing for you, but causes your body harm, and takes hard-earned dollars out of your pocket, you will be wiser. Just read the warning label on your pack of cigarettes and ask yourself: Why do you do it? Do you enjoy your smoker's cough? Do you enjoy poor health attributed to your not having the courage to stop smoking?

A person who smokes a pack of cigarettes a day can save a lot of money. How much money will you save in a year if you quit smoking today? How much money will you save in ten years? A heck of a lot. The money that you spend on cigarettes is better saved or invested. Do the math yourself.

Get a pen or a calculator and determine how much you spend on cigarettes each day, month, and year since you began smoking. The money that you will save from quitting could pay for a trip every year, or a health club membership.

You have the power to change your thoughts about cigarettes. Quitting is easy, and you will do it. It is as simple as saying no to tobacco products and dealing with the withdrawal symptoms. Yeah, it is true that you might experience some nervousness and irritability. You may feel a bit nauseous. You may even get a headache that won't quit for days. But so what? You probably have been through much worse in life.

Remember, if you focus on the fear or the negative, your attempt to quit will be more difficult. If you focus and celebrate quitting because it will save you money, you will have fewer colds, your circulation will improve, your sinus troubles will lessen, and your bad breath, smelly hair, and clothes will be a thing of the past—then it will be easier to quit. Are you admitting that you can't handle a few days of discomfort and irritability? It's no worse than what you feel when you have the flu. The emotional part is being strong and not allowing yourself to smoke again. Once you learn how to control the things in your life that you want, everything becomes possible. No one is making you smoke but yourself. It is not important to think about how difficult it will be to stop smoking, or how much weight you may gain, or what to do when stressful situations arise and you need a cigarette.

You just have to take one step at a time and handle the situations as they come up. You have the strength within you to quit, everyone does. We were all given free will. Some just choose not to take it. You will find the strength, and you will quit smoking. If you want to quit, just tell yourself you will do it, and nothing will stand in your way. It is okay to get angry and upset about your addiction. This is the emotion you need to make sure you never smoke again. Hard work is always painful. It's easier to just give up and slide back into the habit of smoking again after quitting, or never even try to quit.

In this book, I am sharing an incredible amount of information about myself, and at times you may feel as if I'm lecturing you or ask, "What has all this talk to do with quitting smoking?" I could have chosen to exclude my travels to Nepal and Tibet and talk only about the lessons I learned, but this is more than a quit-smoking book. It is also about self-discovery. I have opened my soul to you in order for you to find yourself.

By going inside myself in Nepal, I began to reveal some of my own insecurities and understand some of reasons behind why I do some of the things that I don't want to do. This book is designed to help you rediscover your mind, body, and spirit. You can be a genius with an innovative mind, but if your spirit is not attuned, your knowledge and thoughts are of no use to either the universe or yourself. Your body is, of course, the temple that feeds your mind and spirit. If you choose to take illegal drugs, smoke tobacco, and abuse alcohol and prescribed medication, you will destroy your mind and your spirit. The best way to condition the body is through a balanced diet and exercise. The best way to condition the spirit is through God, meditation, and prayer. The best way to condition the mind is to keep it and your heart open. It is also important to keep your mind active by learning and reading. You have full control to make your life what it was meant to be. Harmony, balance, awareness, and simplicity are the "secrets" to life.

CHAPTER 12

Free Will

Before quitting, I was smoking about two to three packs a day. I realized I could no longer continue abusing my body. I was addicted to nicotine and couldn't quit. The message I want you to understand is the mistakes you make are not important, as long as you do not repeat them. Correct what is wrong and move on. We all have free will. Unlike most animals, we can control our environment and change our conditions to suit our needs. Most importantly, we can also change our thinking to suit our needs and perception. We as humans don't have to act out of instinct. Instead, we can choose to ignore or desire our instinct.

I ran away to Nepal to escape the pressures of the Western world. I came back with a refreshed soul and realized I was responsible about how I felt. The trip to Nepal and Tibet taught me how to forgive and accept life without clinging to past habits and mistakes. I am a nonsmoker and will never allow myself to go back to smoking again!

Paying the tobacco companies to destroy my health was not a smart way to spend my money. Just seeing all the tobacco advertisements and billboards in Nepal was enough to bring back memories of how I was influenced by the Marlboro Man and Joe Camel. How do I know that I will never smoke again after failing repeatedly? I love myself too much to allow myself to smoke again, and I am too proud to give my money away to some company that has absolutely no concern as to whether I live or die.

After Nepal, I knew I would never smoke again. So, I worked on my weight. I joined a health spa and made a commitment to go as often as I could. I usually go three times a week. How did I find the time? Simple: I found a health club that was open twenty-four hours a day, seven days a week. This way I could not make any excuses not to go the gym. When writing the first edition of this book, I was able to get my weight down to 185 pounds from 240 pounds. Now, I am back to 200 pounds and going to the gym less, but I am still conscious of my weight. I didn't enjoy the 24/7 gym, so I quit and joined a fitness club that has a swimming pool and sauna. These activities I enjoy, so they will make me go more frequently. I also bought a mountain bike and go riding for hours. I was a true procrastinator in serious denial about my weight and everything that had to do with cigarettes and eating. It is a shame that I had to travel so far away to realize what is universal and basic common sense: Smoking stinks and is a waste of money. Eating right and exercise will do you good.

My travels in Nepal enabled me to experience emotions I never knew existed. I learned how to be honest with myself, no matter how painful it was. I accepted my addiction and began to fight. But before I could change my mindset, I had to deprogram myself from the years of brainwashing by the tobacco industry and the world of advertising. I had to reprogram my mind to hate cigarettes, although I had a strong craving for *just one more puff.* I knew that if I continued to think negative thoughts about cigarettes, my mind could only believe it. Today I abhor cigarettes and everything about them. Before learning that I was in control of my thoughts, I would have focused on my craving, or on missing tobacco. We will always tend to focus on what we don't have. Instead, I learned how to focus on how fortunate I am to have finally quit, and on not having smoker's breath, yellow teeth, and dirty lungs.

You must get it into your head that smoking is harmful. Just read the warning label on your pack of cigarettes each time you light up. I want you to loathe everything connected with smoking.

Building hatred toward tobacco is necessary to banish your urge for all tobacco products. Through the research that I did, I found that most successful nonsmokers had one thing in common—a loathing for tobacco.

I have developed such strong feelings against cigarettes that I probably couldn't seriously date a smoker, no matter how interesting or attractive she might be. Smoking is nothing more than an addiction. I don't want to breathe it, smell it, or have its fumes in my home or on my clothes. Just the thought of kissing a smoker is repulsive to me.

You can't stay a nonsmoker and still be attached to positive images of tobacco. You only need to know and believe what I am telling you about tobacco products; stop denying the obvious and change your views. Every time I see a smoker, I see a person addicted to a substance, in denial and insecure. How can you like yourself and smoke? You simply can't. I don't want to judge you; this is not my purpose. I just want you to wake up! This is the main reason I wrote this book.

My hope is to help you escape from your addiction to the drug nicotine. Most people are unaware that nicotine is a psychoactive drug—that is, it affects your mind and your behavior along with your soul. So please read on with an open mind. Just let it all sink in. Your mind at times may reject my words and put doubts in your head. This is how one stays addicted to a substance. This is normal. Remember, nicotine affects your behavior and your logic. Just notice it and move on. Fight the urge, and read this book until the end. Stay with it, it's worth it! You don't have to believe every word. You just have to be able to control your mind and its thought processes. Be mindful! I now have inner confidence and know who I am. I understand my weaknesses and my strengths, and I work each day to avoid repeating the mistakes of my past. For the first time, I can say with total confidence that I would never go back to smoking. I am too smart for that, and I simply don't want to harm myself anymore.

Now that I have shared so much of my life to you, I want you to begin your self-discovery, to go inward and look back on your first smoking experience.

Assignment #1: Your first cigarette visualization

I have found through my research after interviewing smokers that a large percentage actually remember their first smoking experience. They also remembered why they began smoking and what insecurities or rebellions led them to start. Now it is your turn to remember your first experience with smoking:

1) Analyze your first experience with smoking.
2) Take some time right now and just recapture your first experience with smoking.
3) Try to remember the place, the people you were with, and how you felt as you took your first puff.
4) It is very important to examine the reasons why you smoked your first cigarette.
5) Was it because of curiosity?
6) Was it because your parent smoked?
7) Was it offered to you?

This is not an assignment to ignore. If you feel a bit tired, then please put the book down until you feel refreshed, so you can complete the assignment. Remember this book is about being mindful. So, if you don't want to do the assignment now, do it when you have time. Close the book and come back when you are ready.

Take as long as you need to examine your first smoking experience. This visualization is important. Quitting smoking for some can be extremely difficult. Nicotine, the chemical found in the tobacco plant, plays a major role in keeping smokers hooked on the habit. Nicotine's physical addiction is just one of the many different reasons smokers can't give up their addiction.

Smoking has been touted more addictive than any drug on the market today. Whether you smoke a cigarette, cigar, pipe, or use snuff or chewing tobacco, I will help you with the physical, emotional, psychological, and spiritual conditions necessary to make you a nonsmoker for the rest of your life. It doesn't have to be so difficult. Just read on! I will work with you to build your inner strength, willpower, and desire needed to throw away your cigarettes and never crave another.

CHAPTER 13

What Exactly Is Nicotine?

Nicotine is an alkaloid found in the leaves of the tobacco plant known as nicotinia tabacum. When nicotine was isolated from tobacco leaves in the early to mid-1800s, scientists began studying its effects on the brain and body. This research eventually revealed that, although tobacco contains thousands of chemicals, the main ingredient that acts on the brain and causes addiction is nicotine. More recent research has shown that the addiction produced by nicotine is extremely powerful and is at least as strong as other drug addictions such as heroin and cocaine.

Nicotine in the brain is responsible for keeping many smokers addicted to the substance, which is known as a psychoactive drug. Such drugs can alter mood, cognitive processes, and behaviors that can cause anxiety and mental tension. Nicotine within the brain also stimulates the productions of other chemicals, hormones, and endorphins, which help smokers control their irritability, reduce social shyness, increase concentration, and minimize insecurities.

When tobacco is smoked, nicotine enters the bloodstream through the lungs or the bloodstream through the mucous membranes of the nose, mouth, and skin. It takes about twelve seconds after inhalation for nicotine to reach the brain. Nicotine's ability to act on the brain is because it has a similar three-dimensional shape to the biochemical acetylcholine. Nicotine works in the body through competition, which is described by the "lock and key" method known as receptor center and neurotransmitter.

Imagine that there are many receptors in your brain waiting for instruction or information to start or complete a task. The neurotransmitter, acetylcholine, attaches to that receptor in the brain to instruct it and the body. Instead, nicotine attaches to the acetylcholine's receptor, thus preventing acetylcholine from binding, and results in an increase in blood pressure and heart rate, along with the production of hormones, other neurotransmitters, and endorphins. Through these mechanisms, nicotine has been known to increase concentration, lower irritability, decrease appetite, and help deal with shyness.

No wonder it is known as the most addictive substance of all time. Nicotine follows the same mechanisms and patterns as cocaine and other stimulants. Nicotine attaches itself to receptors in the brain, interfering with the processes and causing the smoker to feel an initial lift, then a fall, and ultimately destroying the natural order and workings of the brain and nerves. These feelings are associated with the rise and fall of acetylcholine. When nicotine levels drop in the body, the craving begins and the withdrawal symptoms take over until the smoker takes another puff. Then the cycle begins again, and one feels calm, less stressed, and focused. Nicotine ultimately will destroy your nerves. It does give temporary satisfaction, but in reality, the smoker is creating the anxiety by smoking. Nicotine has the power to relieve depression; it helps to suppress fits of anger and to enhance one's short-term memory and concentration. This is why it is so hard to quit. Smokers also need to know that nicotine comes with four thousand other chemicals when inhaled, so you aren't only inhaling nicotine, but you are also breathing in cancer-causing elements. Nicotine is not a miracle drug, but a drug that should be illegal. Nicotine creates chemical imbalance within your brain, and some believe it may actually cause depression. The chemicals within tobacco will also destroy your nerves and circulation, along with killing brain cells.

In summation, nicotine works on a host of other neurotransmitters, such as glutamate (involved in memory and brain cell death), acetylcholine (excitatory when responding to nicotine), gamma aminobutyric acid (a dopamine regulator), serotonin (a mood regulator), and norepinephrine (involved in energy). Nicotine is a strong, powerful brain drug, unlike no other. It has the potential to affect so many different elements within the brain that it is potentially dangerous to the stability of the brain's chemistry and neural network. The "benefits" of tobacco are only temporarily. It makes you feel good. But with most drugs that make you feel good, there are always side effects. So in reality there are no benefits to smoking! Smoking stops your normal pathway from functioning the way it was designed.

Quitting will give you back your life so you are no longer dependent on a drug. Levels of acetylcholine will fall back to normal in a couple of weeks after quitting smoking, and you will actually feel less stress when your body goes back to its natural state. Some of the effects of nicotine include changes in respiration and blood pressure, constriction of arteries, and increased alertness. Many are produced through nicotine's action on the central and peripheral nervous systems. On an agricultural level, nicotine is used as a herbicide known to gardeners and farmers, killing all sorts of insects that ingest the powerful poison.

Here is a fact about your enemy, nicotine... Did you know that it takes only about sixty milligrams of nicotine to instantaneously kill a human? We don't die from nicotine when smoking because you inhale only about two milligrams of it at a time, and the miraculous human body notices it as a poison that can kill you and quickly breaks it down before your next puff. If your body was unable to break down the nicotine from each puff, then puff number thirty would kill you.

Now, why would you willingly want to inhale insecticides? I get very upset at smokers who remain in denial and can't be honest with themselves—smokers who don't believe that smoking is harmful. They are the skeptics of society. They believe the government is taking away their civil rights with the banning of smoking in certain areas. I guess everyone has the right to inhale insecticides if he or she truly wants to, but why would you want to? I am a nonsmoker and I don't want to inhale your smoke even when I'm outside. This is *my* civil right! This is why I fought for banning cigarette smoking in public places in New York. In a report released in 1993, the Environmental Protection Agency noted that "the widespread exposure to environmental tobacco smoke in the United States represents a serious and substantial public health impact." The EPA further concludes that in adults, passive smoke is a Class A (known human) carcinogen responsible for approximately three thousand lung cancer deaths annually in U.S. nonsmokers.

Besides nicotine, cigarette smoke and the components of tobacco consist of more than four thousand compounds, about forty of them extremely serious, including cardiac poisons, cancer-causing agents, and industrial solvents that cause heart disease, strokes, pulmonary and respiratory diseases, cancer, and birth defects.

Tobacco smoke affects you in different ways. When you are exposed to smoke in the environment, it is called involuntary or "passive smoke." There is mainstream smoke, which is inhaled by the smoker. Then there is exhaled smoke, which is breathed out by the smoker. And finally there is side-streams smoke, which consists of substances released from the lit end of the cigarette. The side-stream and the exhaled smoke can have damaging effects known as secondhand smoke. Smokers can also inhale some of their own exhalation if they inhale their exhaled smoke through their nostrils or mouth, thus increasing their risks of smoking-related illnesses.

It has been said that smoking has the power to kill more people in America than heroine, crack, marijuana, cocaine, alcohol, AIDS, automobile accidents, murder, and fire combined. Out of the four thousand-plus chemicals found in tobacco smoke, approximately two hundred or more are known carcinogens. Secondhand smoke is the third leading preventable cause of death in the United States, killing thirty-eight thousand to sixty-five thousand nonsmokers every year. Exposure to secondhand smoke has been linked to asthma, bronchitis, pneumonia, and ear infections in children. Exposure to secondhand smoke has also been noted to increase the risk that infants will die of Sudden Infant Death Syndrome (SIDS). So if you must smoke while reading this book, *don't* do it around those that you care for. There will be a day soon when smokers will be sued for ignoring the demands of nonsmokers. We don't want your smoke. In 2001, an Australian court ruled that a social club was responsible for the throat cancer suffered by one of its waitresses after she was exposed to secondhand smoke while working there. Secondhand smoke is no joke. Don't do it around nonsmokers.

CHAPTER 14

Smoking and Nicotine Addiction

How did we become addicted to nicotine? What led you to try your first cigarette? Did your parents or sibling smoke? Do you believe a gene is responsible for being addicted to nicotine? Are we just products of an ad campaign?

A huge population of smokers started because of the images that were disseminated by the media magazine, television, newspapers, billboards, commercials, and our peers. Just think about it for a while. You had to have some sort of positive image about cigarettes in order for it to become desirable enough to want to try it.

What was it that made you try your first cigarette? Do you remember your first puff? How nasty was that first inhalation? We all experienced the coughing, the dizziness, the teary eyes, and the nausea that accompanied our first cigarette. These autonomic responses to tobacco are natural and normal. They were nothing more than a biological response to reject a substance potentially dangerous to you. Did you remember having similar experiences? If you don't, then try a bit harder.

Why was it, then, if cigarettes tasted so disgusting and displeasing, that you continued to smoke after your first bad experience with tobacco? Pure and simple, you must have had some positive emotion or feeling toward smoking. You might have believed it made you look older or cooler. Whatever the reasons, you would have never smoked your second cigarette if you were not connected to the experience of smoking. For example, if you try a particular food, let's say cabbage, and you absolutely abhor it because it gives you gas and it tastes horrible, you would never eat it again. Now, if you believed that cabbage made you stronger, sexier, and cooler, you may continue to eat it because you believed you would benefit from eating it.

Smoking, on the other hand, at first gave you absolutely no benefits; you coughed, you felt weak, and it gave you a headache. It was supposed to—it is *a poison.* So why did you take your second puff unless you believed it benefited you in some way? You can't say that you enjoyed the taste at first. A person is first drawn to cigarettes by social considerations, such as wanting to seem tough or sophisticated. You continued to smoke because it gave you some sort of reward, and before you knew it, you were addicted.

We as a society are always subjected to media stimulation to encourage us to buy advertised products. Since we were children, the media has bombarded us with subliminal messages through televisions, billboards, magazines, commercials, and movies. These messages told boys and men that smoking would make them cooler, tougher, stronger, macho, and alluring to women. However, they were not aimed only at males. Women were also victims of the brainwashing. The messages geared at them indicated that when women smoked, they became more sophisticated, independent, sexy, glamorous, and alluring to men.

We as a nation have always been influenced by product advertisements. This is not necessarily a bad thing—advertisements help us choose one product over another and bring us diversity. Cigarettes, on the other hand, have been shown to cause cancer. But when a product is as dangerous as cigarettes and alcohol, we must make sure our children are not exposed to the propaganda and hype.

Why do we as consumers continue to buy products that harm? The tobacco companies have been accused of hiding data about tobacco's addictive power and its ability to cause harm. It sounds a bit evil, doesn't it? No one ever said the business world was about being nice. Business is about making money. You don't need a soul to sell a product! However, those who abuse the workings of a system will ultimately pay in the long run. Tobacco industries are now paying for their wrong doings. States have sued the tobacco companies and obtained huge settlements to cover smoking-related illnesses paid by the state via Medicaid.

According to the Associated Press, the tobacco industry has been hit with a lawsuit accusing it of violating the civil rights of black Americans by specifically trying to sell them menthol cigarettes. Their claim states that menthol cigarettes create additional toxic substances not found in nonmenthol cigarettes. They claim also that using the menthol makes it easier for people to smoke longer and inhale deeper. When one looks at the statistics associated with the Surgeon General's report, African Americans account for about 10 percent of all U.S. smokers, and also make up 60 to 70 percent of menthol cigarette consumers.

The tobacco industry has been accused of using marketing techniques to steer men, women, children, and different ethnic groups toward particular brands of cigarettes. Some brands have more toxins than others. We as consumers have followed their commands and bought their products like robots. It was commonplace for cigarette billboards to be posted in the poorest neighborhoods. In more affluent areas, we tend to see more clothing billboards advertisements. Why is it that in certain neighborhoods, it is not cool to smoke anything but Marlboro Reds while in others, Newport and Kool are the only acceptable brands among kids?

We are all victims of advertisement schemes. Just look at the brands you tend to buy. Why do you buy a particular brand of jeans or sneakers? You do it to fit in and be noticed, or to look good. It is as simple as that. Brut 33 and Old Spice were once popular, but try wearing them in the new millennium. It is just not acceptable in our culture to wear outdated brands. The media plays a huge role in your life, whether you believe it or not. I have always had the mindset of being responsible for my own actions, and I am not saying that tobacco companies should not be allowed to advertise, but where do you draw the line? Alcohol kills many of its users by destroying their livers and the lives of many families. Any product known to man, if used obsessively, has the ability to cause harm.

Why is it that we sometimes don't use our brains? Selling tobacco products is a business. We have the right to buy them or not. Many people in business will sell you anything if you are stupid enough to buy it. It is a sad statement, but it is also a true one. The old saying, "Buyer beware" applies here. It is up to the consumer to research and investigate a product.

CHAPTER 15

Biological Dependence and Emotional Replacement

Smoking is no different from any other addiction. It helps one escape reality. Drugs alter your brain chemistry and make you temporarily distant from problems at hand. When one takes cocaine or other drugs, the neurotransmitter, dopamine, rises in the brain for extended periods, resulting in heightened pleasure. According to a study from the Department of Energy at Brookhaven Laboratory, a possible link was found to indicate nicotine addiction can be the result of increased dopamine in the brain, as it is for cocaine and other illegal drugs.

Dopamine is thought to be responsible for basic human experiences of pleasure. The dopamine rush is the same feeling a drug addict experiences when using crack or cocaine. It is the same feeling some people experience when eating a chocolate bar or ice cream. It is also known as the "runner's high." It is the same feeling that you can experience from being hugged by someone you care about. This link would be responsible for the rewarding and reinforcing behavior found in smokers.

Another link to the pleasure neurotransmitter dopamine and cigarettes is an enzyme, monoamine oxidase B (MAO B), which was discovered by researchers to be about 40 percent less in smokers than in nonsmokers or ex-smokers. This means there must be something in the four thousand-plus chemicals in tobacco smoke, which lowers the levels of MAO B. Lower levels of this enzyme lead to increased levels of dopamine in the brain. So it is true that smoking does actually make you less anxious and does have the ability to alter your mood—but at what cost?

Scientists are looking at various ways to reduce or help cravings of nicotine. Companies are working on vaccines to help the cravings for cigarettes by preventing the nicotine molecule from entering the brain. If nicotine never enters the brain, then the craving to smoke will end. You will no longer want to inhale four thousand-plus chemicals without the nicotine affecting your brain chemistry. Other scientists are working on altering the way brain cells talk to one another: GVG, or gamma vinyl-GABA, is another method that may help smokers quit. GVG is involved with reducing the level of dopamine in the region of the brain that is involved with nicotine and cocaine addiction, as noted by the Brookhaven National Laboratory.

People who smoke cigarettes use tobacco to maintain nicotine levels in the brain, primarily to avoid the negative effects of nicotine withdrawal, but also to modulate their mood. The ability to quit can be difficult for many. If you are one of those who have severe withdrawals when attempting to quit, I would suggest that you speak with your physician to suggest Zyban or another medication to help deal with the withdrawal symptoms. The active agent in Zyban is bupropion hydrochloride, which is also used in the antidepressant drug Wellbutrin. If you also fear that you will gain weight when you quit, and you are already overweight, talk to your doctor about a weight-loss program or even schedule an appointment with a nutritionist. There is some evidence that Zyban may attenuate the weight gain normally associated with quitting smoking. Zyban and other antidepressants may be extremely successful for those who have had difficulty quitting in the past, because these drugs work on some of the same brain chemicals that nicotine affects.

Remember, you must plan your quitting. This is extremely important. If you know it will be difficult to quit cold turkey because of depression and the possibility of gaining weight, talk with your doctor as soon as possible. Make a schedule with your doctor to quit now. If you are in good health and you believe you don't need pills to help you quit, or to help you lose weight, then that is great. This is how I did it. I spoke with my doctor about exercising, to make sure my heart was in good shape, and I jogged every other day when I quit. This helped to balance my brain chemistry to a natural level, so I did not miss nicotine or the withdrawal symptoms associated with nicotine.

Another reason people become addicted to a substance is because something is usually missing from their lives. The substance is then used as a replacement for whatever is lacking. The replacement causes the brain's chemistry to change through increased dopamine levels and the satisfaction is temporarily felt. This can be as simple as buying something new, like a gadget, to boost one's mood.

This replacement substance does not last long and you still require it to feel elevated again. Thus a vicious cycle begins. One cannot be truly happy inside and continue to smoke with all we now know about tobacco and smoking-related illnesses. Happy people would not play Russian roulette with their lives! The chemical dopamine gives you that temporary relief of satisfaction. Whatever the fact may be, you can combat it! Your brain has the power to do anything you feed it. Fortunately for you, quitting is not difficult. Once you know the facts and accept them, and with a bit of courage, you will stop your habit.

Right now, I want you to get prepared to give up smoking. I will reveal your last day of smoking, and smoking for you will be a thing of the past. So if you believe that you may need help with depression when you quit, please talk to your doctor, *now*. You need to also talk to your physician if you feel you need help with dealing with the cravings and how to deal with weight. There is some evidence that suggests that smokers may be more successful with quitting when on antidepressants, such as Zyban.

By no means do I want you to use any form of nicotine replacement therapies. No gums or patches. I want you to quit without using nicotine or weaning yourself off nicotine. Research tends to show that most people are successful at remaining nonsmokers for the rest of their lives by quitting entirely on their own. I tried almost everything to help me quit: nicotine gum and lozenges, hypnosis, nicotine spray, acupuncture, herbs, etc., and they all failed. I have even tried antidepressants, and they were successful when quitting, but when I stopped taking them, I still needed to be able to cope with life. I was back smoking within three months because of stress triggers. Your urge to quit smoking must come from within. This is why I introduced you to the idea of meditation, which works on the spiritual level. Meditation has the ability to calm your mind, body, and spirit, which will help you deal with stress.

There is no pill on the market to help a person with their drive or will. The magic is within you. You must learn instead to deal with why you feel the need to smoke. Do you smoke when you are nervous? Do you smoke to curb your appetite? We must deal with the habit. We must also deal with the triggers that get us to restart smoking when we have quit and said goodbye. My triggers were always stress-related.

This is what this book is about—awareness and truth. Cigarette smoking is one of the worst things you can possibly do to your body.

CHAPTER 16

Constituents of Tobacco Products and Their Smoke

Here is a *partial* list of the substances and chemical compounds in the tobacco, the exhaled smoke, and the filter of a cigarette:

1,1-Dimethylhydrazine; 1,3 Butadiene; 1,4-Benzenediol; 1-Aminonapthaline; 1-Carvone; 1-Phenyl-1-Propanol; 2,3-Diethylpyrazine; 2,3-Dimethylpyrazine; 2,6-Dimethoxyphenol; 2,6-Dimethylpyrazine; 2-Aminonaphthalene; 2-Cyclopentanedione; 2-Decenal; 2-Ethyl-1-Hexanol, 2-Ethyl-3-Methylpyrazine; 2-Methylbutyraldehyde; 2-Methylhexanoic Acid; 2-Methylpyrazine; 2-Methylvaleric Acid; 2-Nitropropane; 2-Pentylpyridine; 2-Phenyl-2-Butenal; 3-Aminobiphenyl, 3-Hexenoic Acid; 3-Methyl-1-Cyclopentadecanone; 3-Methylbutyraldehyde; 3-Methylbutyrate; 3-Methylpentanoic Acid; 3-Methylthiopropionate; 3-Phenyl-1-Propanol; 3-Phenylpropionaldehyde; 3-Phenylpropyl Acetate; 4-Aminobiphenyl; 4-Aminobiphenyl Benzene; 4-Ethylbenzaldehyde; 4-Heptenal; 4-Methyl-1-Phenyl-2-Pentanone; 4-Methyl-5-Thiazoleethanol; 4-(Methylnitrosamino)-1-(3-Pyridyl)-1-Butanone; 4-(Methylnitrosamino)-1-(3-pyridyl)-1-Butanone; 4-Aminobiphenyl 4-Methylacetophenone; 4-Methylpentanoic 2-Octenal; 4-Methylphenol (p), 4-Phenyl-3-Buten-2-Ol; 4-Trans-Decadienal; 5-Ethyl-3-Hydroxy-4-Methyl-2(5H)-Furanone; 5-Methyl-2-Phenyl-2-Hexenal; 5-Methyl-2-Thiophenecarboxaldehyde; 5-Methylchrysene; 5-Methylquinoxaline; 7H-Dibenz[c,g]carbazole; Acetaldehyde; Acetate copolymer; Acetic Acid; Acetone; Acetronitrile; Acrolein; Acrylonitrile; Acylonitride; Aluminum; Aminobiphenyl; Ammonia; Anabasine; Aniline; Anthracenes; Argon; Arsenic; Benz(a)anthracene; Benzene; Benzo(k)fluoranthene; Benzo[a]pyrene; Benzo[b]fluoranthene; Benzo[j]fluoranthene; Benzo[k]fluoranthene; Beta-Carotene; Beta-Caryophyllene Oxide; Beta-Caryophyllene; Bicarbonate; Boric Acid; Butadiene; Butane; Butyraldehyde; Cadmium; Calcium Carbonate; Campesterol; Carbolic Acid; Carbon Dioxide; Carbon Monoxide; Catechol; Cationic Starch; Cellulose Fiber; Chamomile Flower Oil and Extract; Chromium; Chromium;2-Naphthylamine; Chrysene;

Cinnamon Leaf Oil; Cinnamyl Cinnamate; Cinnamyl cis-3-Hexenyl Formate; Cinnamyl Alcohol; Cinnamyl Propionate; Citronella Oil; Citronellyl Isobutyrate; Citronellyl Butyrate; Copper; Cresylic Acid (mixture); Crotonaldehyde; Crotonaldehyde; Cyclotenes; DDT/Dieldrin; Decanoic Acid; Dehydromenthofurolactone; Dibenz(a, h)acridine; Dibenz(a, h)anthracene; Dibenzo(a,i)pyrene; Dibenz[a,h]acridine; Dibenz[a,j]acridine; Dibenzo(a,i)pyrene; Dibenzo(a,I)pyrene; Dibenzo(c, g)carbazole; Dibenz[a,h]acridine; Dibenz[a,j]acridine;Diethyl Sebacate; Diethyl Malonate; Dimenthylhydrazine; Eloxylated Sorbitan; Endrine; Ethylcarbamate; Ethylene-vinyl; Etylmethylnitrosamine; Fluoranthenes; Fluorenes; Formaldehyde; Formic Acid; Fumeric Acid; Furan; Galbanum Oil; gamma-Dodecalactone; Gamma-Octalactone; Geraniol; Glycerol Triacetin; Hexamine; Hexyl 2-Methylbutyrate; Hexyl Acetate; Hexyl Alcohol; Hydrazine; Hydrogen Cyanide; Hydrogen Sulfide; Hydroquinone; Hydroxybenzene; Indeno[1,2,3-cd]pyrene, Indole; Isoprene; Lead; Limonene; Linoleic Acid; Linseed Alkyd Varnish; m + p-Cresol; m-Dihydroxybenzene; Magnesium; Menthol; Mercury; Meta-Dimethoxybenzene; Methane; Methyinitrosamino; Methyl Ethyl Ketone; Methyl Benzoate; Methyl 2-Pyrrolyl Ketone; Methyl Anisate; Methyl Anthranilate; Methyl-alpha-Ionone; Methyl-trans-2-Butenoic Acid; Methylamine; Methylamineethylchrysene; Methylcyclopentenolone; Methylpyrrolidine; N-Nitrosoanabasine (NAB); Hydrogen cyanide; Indeno[1,2,3-cd]pyrene; N-Nitrosoanatabine (NAT); N-Nitrosonornicotine (NNN); N-Nitrosodiethanolamine; N-Nitrosonornicotine; Nickel; Nicotine; Nitric oxide; Nitrobenzene; Nitropropane; Nitrosamines; Nitrosonornicontine; Nitrous oxide; N-Nitrosodiethanolamine N-Nitrosodiethylamine; N-Nitrosodimethylamine; N-Nitrosomethylethylamine; N-Nitrosomorpholine; N-Nitrosomethylethylamine; N-Nitrosomorpholine; N-Nitrosonornicotine (NNN); N-Nitrosopyrrolidine; N-Nitrosopyrrolidine; Naphthalene; Naphthylamine; Neophytadienes; o-Cresol; Octyl Isobutyrate; Olibanum Oil;

Opoponax Oil and Gum; Orange 2-Octynoate; Ortho-Toluidine; Oxybenzene; p-Dihydroxybenzene; p-Hydroxyphenol; Ortho-Toluidine; Palmarosa Oil; Palmitic Acid; para-Dimethoxybenzene; para-Dimethylbenzyl Alcohol; para-Ethoxybenzaldehyde; para-Ethylphenol; para-Methylanisole; para-TolylAcetaldehyde; para-Tolyl Isobutyrate; para-Tolyl Acetate; Parsley Seed Oil; Patchouli Oil; Pepper Oil; Peppermint Oil; Phenenthyl Alcohol; Phenethyl Butyrate; Phenethyl Cinnamate; Phenethyl Acid; Phenol; Phenylacetaldehyde; Phenylacetic Acid; Phenylmethylester; Phosphoric Acid; Polonium-210 (Radon); Polyglycol; Polyvinyl Alcohol; Propionaldehyde; Pyridine; Pyrocatechol; Pyroligneous Acid and Extract; Pyrrole; Pyruvic Acid; Quinoline;Resorcinol; Rhodinol; Rose Absolute and Oil; Rosemary Oil; Rum Ether; Sodium Carbonate; Sodium Chloride; Sodium Citrate; Sorbitan; Styrene; Sulfide; Tar; Terpinolene; Terpinyl Acetate; Thiamine 1-Decanl; Titanium; Tobacco; Toluene; trans -2-Heptenal; trans-2-Hexenoic Acid; Quinoline; Urethane (EthylCarbamate); Urethane; Vinyl Chloride; and Water.

Here is a list of some of the well-known substances that are known to be **dangerous**:

1,1-DIMETHYLHYDRAZINE. This chemical is known to cause convulsions in animals. Exposure can also cause liver damage in humans from chronic exposure to 1,1-Dimethylhydrazine. Exposure is usually from rocket fuel.

2-NITROPROPANE. It is a solvent used in inks, paints, and varnish. Exposure can cause headaches, anorexia, nausea, and vomiting. Known to cause severe liver and kidney damage.

4-AMINOBIPHENYL. It is no longer used in the workplace, has been used as a rubber antioxidant and a dye intermediate. Smokers were found to have higher levels of the breakdown of 4-aminobiphenyl in their blood than of nonsmokers. 4-aminobiphenyl is known to cause cancer in humans. It is widely known in the scientific community as a potent bladder carcinogen. There is no known safe level of 4-aminobiphenyl. Short-term exposure is known to produce headaches, lethargy, cyanosis, and blood in the urine.

1-AMINONAPHTHALENE. Used in dyes, rubber, and weed control. It has been shown to cause lung and liver damage, and leukemia in animals. Absorption occurs both by inhalation and through the skin.

2-AMINONAPHTHALENE. Banned or restricted use in industry, it is known to cause cancer in humans. There is no safe level of this substance.

4-AMINOBIPHENYL. No longer produced on a commercial scale because it is known to cause cancer in humans, especially cancer of the bladder. There is no safe level of this chemical.

ACETALDEHYDE. The main industrial use of acetaldehyde includes silvering of mirrors. Studies have shown that acetaldehyde causes cancer in animals and may cause cancer in humans. Known to irritate the eyes, skin, and respiratory tract of humans and animals. In animal studies, it was shown that acetaldehyde interfered with the exchange of nutrients from the mother to the placenta, resulting in growth retardation, malformation, delayed bone growth, and death of the fetus.

ACROLEIN. Main uses are herbicides and tear gas. Long-term effects include inflammation of the lungs, liver, and kidney. Acrolein is a strong irritant of the eyes and upper respiratory system of humans.

ACRYLONITRILE. It is used as a fumigant for tobacco. This chemical is suspected to cause cancer in humans. There is evidence to suggest that chronic exposure may result in deformation of the fetus and offspring.

BENZENE. Was used in industry to manufacture inks, rubber, lacquers, and paint remover. Known to cause cancer in humans. Prolonged exposure is likely to cause leukemia. Benzene is a highly toxic substance.

BENZO[A]PYRENE. "B[A]P" is suspected to cause cancer in humans. There is a significant correlation between B[A]P exposure and skin cancer, dermatitis, respiratory disease, and emphysema.

CADMIUM. Most cadmium used in the United States today is obtained as a byproduct of the smelting of zinc, lead, or copper ores. Smokers have twice as much cadmium in their bodies than nonsmokers. Long-term exposure to the substance has been linked to kidney stone formation, bronchiolitis, and emphysema.

CARBON MONOXIDE. It's a molecule that replaces oxygen in your body. It is one of the byproducts of smoking, as is the exhaust from your car. Carbon monoxide is so dangerous that without ventilation, one would die within minutes of breathing in this deadly gas. The math is quite simply. The more and longer you smoke, the higher percentage of carbon monoxide is in your blood, resulting in less oxygen to your cells and brain. The brain thrives on oxygen, and every cell in the body needs it to survive. Reducing oxygen by any means can only do harm.

CATECHOL. Main use in industry is rubber dye, insecticides, and photography. Catechol, when inhaled with benzo [a] pyrene (also found in tobacco smoke), is cocarcinogenic. High doses of Catechol causes increased blood pressure, upper respiratory tract irritation, kidney damage, and convulsions.

CRESOL. Mainly used in disinfectants, synthetic resins, dyes, fumigants, and explosives. Cresol is known to promote tumors in mice. Long-term exposure causes headache, nausea, vomiting, elevated blood pressure, impaired kidney function, blood calcium imbalance, and marked tremors in humans.

FORMALDEHYDE. The main uses of formaldehyde in industry include fertilizer, dyes, disinfectants, germicides, preservatives, and embalming fluid. Formaldehyde is suspected of causing cancer in humans. It occurs naturally at 0.12 to 0.38 parts per billion (ppb). Side-stream smoke increases this by 0.23 to 0.27 parts per million (ppm), a 1000+ increase. Long-term exposure at levels greater than 0.1 ppm appears to be a risk for cancers of the lung, pharynx, buccal cavity, liver, bone, skin, prostate gland, bladder, kidney, and eye; leukemia; and Hodgkin's disease. Formaldehyde exposure greater than 0.22 ppm is linked to respiratory symptoms such as cough, phlegm, chronic bronchitis, asthma, shortness of breath, and chest colds. Human eyes are sensitive to formaldehyde at concentrations of 0.01 ppm, and are irritated by formaldehyde at concentrations of 0.05 to 0.5 ppm.

HYDROGEN CYANIDE. The main uses of hydrogen cyanide in industry include fumigation as an insecticide. Hydrogen cyanide causes nasal irritation, confusion, headache, dizziness, weakness, and nausea in humans at moderate doses; at higher doses, it causes asthenia, vertigo, weight loss, and gastrointestinal problems.

HYDRAZINE. Confirmed carcinogen with neoplastigenic and tumorigenic data. Affects include ingestion paresthesia, somnolence, nausea, or vomiting

INDENO[1,2,3-CD]PYRENE. A deadly human poison, by ingesting it causes cardiac arrhythmia, hallucinations, hypoglycemia, convulsions, and thyroid malfunction.

LEAD. The main uses of lead in industry include alloys (solder, bronze, brass), paint pigments, storage batteries, glass, plastics, and ceramics. Lead is known to cause cancer in animals and may cause cancer in humans. Lead is toxic and soluble in body fluids when inhaled and lead poisoning effects on the brain may not be reversible. Lead exposure affects the development of fetuses. Children exposed to high levels of lead in the womb have been found to have developmental defects such as depressed intellectual development.

NICKEL. The main uses of nickel in industry include production of stainless steel, alloys, electroplating, coinage, and alkaline batteries. Nickel has been confirmed to cause cancer in humans.

NICOTINE. The main uses of nicotine in industry (besides tobacco) include insecticides (now mostly banned) and as tranquilizing darts for wildlife. Freebase nicotine in tobacco smoke is absorbed almost instantly by inhalation ingestion and skin contact. Nicotine concentrates in the brain, kidney, stomach mucosa, adrenal medulla, nasal mucosa, and salivary glands. Studies show that nicotine exposure can result in seizures, vomiting, depressions of the central nervous system, growth retardation, developmental toxicity in fetuses, and pre-term birth with reduced body weight and brain development in animals. Mild nicotine poisoning in humans results in the following symptoms: vomiting, diarrhea, increase in respiration, heart rate, blood pressure, headache, dizziness, and neurological stimulation.

ORTHO-TOLUIDINE. Confirmed carcinogen with experimental neoplastigenic and tumorigenic data. Human systemic effects by inhalation: urine volume increases, hematuria, and blood methemoglobinemia. Can produce headache, weakness, difficulty in breathing, air hunger, psychic disturbances, and marked irritation of the kidneys and bladder.

PHENOL. The main industrial uses of phenol include chemicals and drugs, disinfectants, and germicidal applications. Studies have shown phenol to be toxic to the respiratory, cardiovascular, hepatic, renal, and neurological systems of animals. Higher doses may damage the lungs and central nervous system and induce convulsions in humans.

PYRIDINE. The main industrial uses of pyridine include solvents, pesticides, and resins. Exposure to pyridine results in an increased production of blood platelets. Longer exposure causes nausea headache, insomnia, nervousness, and abdominal discomfort in humans.

QUINOLINE. The main industrial uses of quinoline include insecticides, herbicides, corrosion inhibitors, and preservation of anatomical specimens. Quinoline causes genetic mutations and therefore may increase your risk of cancer. Repeated exposure damages the retina of the eye and affects vision. Repeated exposure may damage the liver. Quinoline is irritating to the eyes, nose, throat, and bronchial tubes, and may cause sore throat, nosebleeds, cough, and phlegm.

STYRENE. Styrene is used predominantly in the production of polystyrene and resins. It has been found to cause headaches, ocular and conjunctival irritation, diminished reaction time, fatigue, dizziness, nausea, reduced attention and manual dexterity, and reductions in color discrimination in humans.* Reproductive effects of styrene include a possible incidence of increase of spontaneous abortion and the number of abnormal sperm.

TOLUENE. The highest concentrations of toluene usually occur in indoor air from the use of common household products (paints, paint thinners, and adhesives) and cigarette smoke. The central nervous system is the primary target organ for toluene toxicity in both humans and animals. Toluene is highly toxic and is a possible reproductive toxin. Inhaled, toluene appears in blood circulation within ten seconds and accumulates in body fat. Long-term, low-level exposure results in headaches, lassitude, loss of appetite, disturbances in menstruation, and reductions in intelligence and psychomotor skills. Higher exposure may cause encephalopathy, headache, depression, lassitude, impaired coordination, transient memory loss, impaired reaction time, dizziness, nasal discharge, drowsiness, and metallic taste in the mouth. The main uses of toluene in industry include rubbers, oils, resins, adhesives, inks, detergents, dyes, and explosives.

TOBACCO-SPECIFIC NITROSAMINES (NNN) is a carcinogenic tobacco-specific nitrosamine (TSNA) found only in tobacco products. NNN is formed from nicotine directly and is the most abundant cancer causing TSNA. NNN is a yellow, oily liquid that is known to cause nose, throat, lung, and digestive tract cancer in animals. NNN may cause reproductive damage in humans. There is no safe level of exposure to this substance.

NNK [(4-methylnitrosamino)-1-(3-pyridyl)-1-butanone] is a carcinogenic tobacco-specific nitrosamine (TSNA) found only in tobacco products. NNK is a powerful lung carcinogen that induces tumors of the lung.

NAT (N-Nitrosoanatabine) is a possibly carcinogenic tobacco specific nitrosamine (TSNA) found only in tobacco products.

POLONIUM-210 (Radon). This material is deposited in the lungs and has been considered a major causative agent in the high incidence of lung cancer found in uranium miners.

VINYL CHLORIDE. This is a confirmed human carcinogen causing liver and blood tumors. Human reproduction is affected by inhalation resulting in changes in spermatogenesis.

With this list, I don't want to mislead you and tell you that all of these chemicals exist at one time. Some do and others don't. Some of the chemicals listed are highly unstable and exist for no longer than a millisecond, others may exist no longer than a microsecond, and still others are in such low concentrations that they may have no significant effect. This is where you need to use your common sense. How can so much bad be good for you?

CHAPTER 17

Advocates of Smokers

Advocates of tobacco maintain that this list is misleading, since most of the substances in tobacco smoke exist for only a millisecond and then vanish. They also state that the concentrations of these chemicals are so low that they simply cannot affect the human system. Sorry, but how can more than four thousand chemicals not have some sort of an effect on your health? Are they saying that these chemicals are instead beneficial to a smoker's health? There are a lot of chemicals within tobacco smoke and no matter how minute they are as byproducts, who in their right mind would intentionally inhale such toxins?

For instance, advocates of smoking state that the U.S. Food and Drug Administration (FDA) is misleading the world into believing smoking is dangerous. These people believe that smoking is beneficial. Their main argument relates to the increased levels of dopamine in the brain caused by cigarette smoking, and they say it is actually beneficial, that increased levels of acetylcholine and dopamine in the brain have been shown to increase alertness and concentration. Advocates of smoking actually claim these heightened neurotransmitters in the brain can also reduce your chances of Alzheimer's disease, and lower the risk of Parkinson's disease. Nicotine may one day provide a powerful tool for scientists in brain research. However, this is not the point.

The point is that tobacco and its smoke contain more than four thousand chemicals, and more than two hundred of them are known to cause cancer or some type of harm to the human system. I remember clearly in 1995 that Philip Morris had to recall nearly eight billion cigarettes, when the chemical methyl-isothiocyanate was found in the cigarette's filter. Luckily, the company acted quickly, and it was reported that only seventy-two persons were afflicted with illness at the time of the recall.

The cells in our body are extremely sensitive to foreign matter. One would be foolish to believe that inhaling four thousand-plus chemicals could be beneficial. Smokers claim to have a right to smoke when and where they want—this is a free country. Nonsmokers fight for their rights, stating that they have the right to a smoke-free environment, free from pollutants. The war between smokers and nonsmokers has become prominent in courtrooms around the world. Courts have ruled in favor of nonsmokers and have ordered awards of disability pay because of tobacco smoke in the workplace.

In Europe, it is estimated that some five hundred thousand deaths every year are caused by smoking-related illnesses. And at least 630,000 in India, ten thousand in South Africa, twenty-three thousand in Australia, thirty thousand in Canada, nineteen thousand in Venezuela, and about four hundred thousand in the United States. It is no wonder smoking is a major cause of illness and premature death and responsible for as much as 9 percent of all lung cancer cases, 75 percent of chronic bronchitis, and 25 percent of ischaemic heart disease in men under sixty-five. Cigarette smoking kills!

We cannot know all the effects of the four thousand-plus chemicals found in tobacco smoke. Some may actually be beneficial, but we definitely know that others cause cancers in humans and are definitely poisonous. These numbers are always changing. The FDA is constantly banning potentially dangerous substances, such as ephedra, an herbal substance that many use for weight loss. Why don't we ban tobacco, since it causes more deaths than car accidents, AIDS, and murder combined?

The powerful tobacco industry is a multi-billion-dollar business with strong lobbyists in Washington, supports the economies of a number of states (and foreign countries where tobacco is grown and exported to the United States), and generates substantial tax revenue for these corporate entities. So we will probably never see tobacco banned in this country, even though ethically it should be. Nicotine creates a fatal dependence, which ultimately results in degrees of disease and possibly death. Since it will likely never be banned, we should *at least* have tougher laws against selling tobacco to minors, as well as more specific, punishing laws against the proliferation of secondhand smoke.

Recent studies have suggested that within the four thousand-plus chemicals, there are about sixty chemicals, including arsenic and benzene, that may actually accelerate the group of pre-existing tumors, according to John Cooke of Stanford University School of Medicine in California. For those who regularly inhale others' smoke—which includes those who work in bars, restaurants and other business or social situations where smoking is allowed, or those who live with smokers, including children who are forced to endure the smoke of their parents, especially in the confinement of cars—generally have a 20 to 30 percent greater risk of contracting lung cancer or heart disease.

CHAPTER 18

Research and Statistics

I could have written and quoted pages of research about smoking-related illnesses, but what I want you to do instead is use your own common sense. Some things in life don't need to be analyzed to understand their effects. One does not have to be a research scientist to know that inhaling poisonous chemicals is harmful to you. People who think otherwise are really fooling themselves and are in serious denial! It is really simple—if you expose your lungs and brain to harmful chemical gases repeatedly, some amount of damage will result. I don't intend to be rude or insult your intelligence, but if you can't come to this conclusion yourself and realize that you are acting self-destructively when you smoke, then you may need some sort of counseling to determine why you allow yourself to be a victim to tobacco—and worse, why you pay the tobacco companies to *deliberately* cause you harm. Is this logical to you?

I want you to realize that smoking is no joke! Our mind has an incredible way of blocking out the stuff we don't want to hear or ignore. You can't imagine how your life will begin to change if you just start thinking a bit more about the reasons behind the stupid things we do. Smoking is idiotic. You get no nutrients from it, and it contains poisons, such as lead, ammonia, and arsenic. Don't become a victim of advertisement schemes to keep you hooked to a habit.

Today, smoking is becoming social unacceptable, but the tobacco companies are smarter and wiser. They have paid celebrities to advertise their product. Pop singers and action stars are being paid to smoke cigars to reflect a new chic image. We behave like robots and absorb the media influence, and bang it is now glamorous to smoke cigars. In New York City, I have seen women, men, and children on the street smoking cigars. This is not glamorous or cool at all. It looks absolutely ridiculous!

I look at these people, knowing they are ruled by the media, who think it is chic or hip because stars such as Demi Moore, Arnold Schwarzenegger, Bruce Willis, Jack Nicholson, Madonna, Sylvester Stallone, Vanessa Williams, Claudia Schiffer, and others have made it cool to smoke cigars. There is nothing more unattractive than a woman smoking a cigar!

Just think, who changed our perception about the filthy practice of women smoking cigars? Some of the more glamorous, sexy stars who have been portrayed smoking cigars include Ellen Barkin, Sandra Bernhard, Demi Moore, Ellen Degeneres, Linda Evangelista, Lauren Hutton, Julianne Moore, and Sharon Stone, to name only a few. We all know that Madonna is known for doing outlandish things; I remember when I saw her smoke a cigar on the "Late Show with David Letterman," thinking how stupid it was. I have seen her in magazines, movies, calendars, and videos promoting cigar smoking to her fans. So what's cool about filming a video or being on a talk show smoking? Cigar smoking is a known risk factor for certain cancers and for chronic obstructive pulmonary disease (COPD). There is nothing cool or fashionable about smoking cigars. It is well established that cigar smoking causes cancer in the oropharynx and the upper aerodigestive tract, including the larynx and esophagus. The FDA attempted to help with banning the many types of advertising and promotion of tobacco—billboards, print advertisements, direct mail, promotional items, and sponsored events to children. Now we have movie stars, singers, and sports athletes promoting tobacco.

Vanessa Williams told People magazine in the March 2000 issue that "smoking cigars relaxes me, more women should try it."

No, I don't think so, Vanessa. Exercise and meditation relaxes. Nicotine is a drug. Don't push your habit on America! While the vast majority of our population officially frown at taking drugs, both legal and illegal, we not only accept smoking, we actually encourage it by our general acceptance. I guess Vanessa doesn't know how damaging smoking is; why else would she publicly tell people that they should smoke cigars to relax them? Not only is smoking dangerous to our body, it also yellows the teeth and ages the skin. I guess this is why Vanessa does commercials for Proactiv and talks publicly about how bad her skin is. Could it be because of her smoking habit?

Scientists believe that smokers are three times as likely to develop premature wrinkling caused by smoking, which can show up in people as young as 20 years old. The four thousand-plus chemicals in tobacco smoke interfere with microvasculature pathways which nourish your skin with oxygen rich blood. Scientists in Europe have discovered that smoking triggers matrix metalloproteinase 1 (MMP-1), an enzyme that destroys collagen. Thus smoking destroys the building blocks of your skin, causing sagging and wrinkles. Rich people can pay thousands of dollars in plastic surgery and inject collagen into their skin (how repulsive), along with teeth whiteners or caps, to fix up what smoking has done to their skin and teeth, but they can't stop it from causing them cancer. Smoking sucks in a number of ways!

I am not writing this book to judge you or to blame superstars for your habit. Nor am I trying to blame the tobacco company. I am just trying to get you, as a smoker, to understand that smoking is not natural. Smoking is an unnatural act to our biological system. It destroys our cells. I started smoking for the same reasons you did. I got suckered into believing that smoking would change or improve my image. I believed the hype. Then I became addicted and couldn't quit, so I lived in constant denial telling my family and friends that I enjoyed smoking.

Smoking does not make sense. It is a slow suicide. The reduction of available oxygen can be easily witnessed by asking a two-pack-a-day smoker to jog with a nonsmoker. I realized this when I attempted to trek in Nepal. I never felt so out of shape in my life. I saw men and women much older than me in better shape than I was. They were able to trek up the mountain without being out of breath, and their pace was also much faster than mine. In my thirties, I expected to be in perfect shape, but I was out of breath within my first hour of walking.

Smoking takes a toll on your lungs, heart, and entire body. You do not need a degree in science to understand how toxic substances can cause havoc on a biological system. Protobacco advocates have been quoted saying that the chemicals found in tobacco smoke also exist in everyday products such as bleach, car exhaust fumes, chemical pesticides, barbecuing, and coffee filters, so why is everyone focusing on tobacco? They are absolutely right, but who in their right mind would intentionally inhale these fumes into their body? I have never seen anyone inhale fumes from a car or from a barbecue grill, or willingly drink bleach.

These protobacco freaks speak utter nonsense and they are also in denial. This is what addiction does—it causes people to abandon good common sense. Even if the chemicals listed previously are in minuscule amounts, why would any human being in their right mind inhale such garbage? We have so much pollution around us already from the air we breathe, in our water, and the food that we eat—why add such a poisonous factor to the list?

Strive for health. Don't gamble with your health, or that of others, by smoking. The fumes from cigarette exhalation and the smoke from lit cigarettes are extremely dangerous. Eighty percent of all cases of lung cancer in America are believed to be directly related to cigarette smoke. Passive smoke affects others, and also affects our children. Passive smoke has lead to an increase in the incidence of upper respiratory infections in early childhood and elevated incidence of childhood asthma.

I know a couple who have two children, both under age six. Each child suffers from asthma. The couple smokes more than two packs a day in their home and in their car while the children are present. I hate to scream "child abuse," but children are innocent at that age and cannot yet speak for themselves, even if they begin to realize that smoke is making them cough or make their eyes water. There really *should* be a law against smoking around minors.

Does the government have the right to protect its citizens from potentially dangerous substances? Studies have found a link giving clues to lung cancer among nonsmokers. Approximately 17 percent of lung cancers among this group can be attributed to high levels of exposure to tobacco smoke in the home during childhood and adolescence. Studies have also shown that children ranging from five to twenty years of age show a positive relation between parental tobacco smoking and the frequency of respiratory illnesses.

It simply amazes me how self-destructive humans can be. Not only does smoking cause the smoker harm, but it also causes harm to those in the same environment as the smoker. Why would anyone smoke around children and people that they love? I say this easily today, but I was no different. I was also addicted to tobacco and ignored all the warnings. This is how *strong a hold* nicotine can have over you, just as heroin has a hold over a junkie. Some people would rather cause damage to their children and loved ones by smoking around them than believe secondhand smoke is dangerous. Secondhand smoke is dangerous! Smoke—whether it comes from a barbecue, the exhaust of a car's pipe, a chimney, or from a lit cigarette—smoke is smoke and it does not belong indoors and in our lungs!

Now that you are aware of some of the substances found in environment tobacco smoke (ETS) and how they are actually harming you, you need to ask yourself, is it worth the risk to continue to smoke? To begin your journey, you have to start believing that smoking is dangerous. You have to believe that smoking can harm everyone who breathes in or inhales the byproducts of tobacco. Accepting your addiction and realizing how dangerous smoking can be to you and others is vital to becoming a nonsmoker. Now you need to start breaking the bonds between you and your feelings toward smoking.

People who smoke say they enjoy cigarettes because it seems to calm their nerves. Others claim it gives them something to do with their hands. Some even say they smoke socially in order to combat shyness; smoking makes them feel more at ease. Smoking does have the ability to calm and give satisfaction to its users. If it did not, it would not be labeled a drug. Smoking is also a habit, something one does over and over until it becomes natural to one's being. At first, smoking actually gives its users no benefits whatsoever. There are no feelings of satisfaction, enjoyment, or comfort. It basically takes a year or more for smokers to develop a sense of satisfaction and enjoyment from tobacco products. One of the main reasons behind this is the change in brain chemistry in relationship to dopamine levels. Knowing the truth, we are able to reason and investigate this aspect of our lives using our mind, instead of the impaired, addictive mind containing nicotine. We can then abandon the false views that we hold about smoking and the fear of letting go. We gain confidence in the path and our ability to quit.

CHAPTER 19

Why We Smoke

1. Taste.

Out of habit, you have become so used to the taste of tobacco, that after a year you actually forgot how horrible cigarettes actually taste. Those four thousand-plus chemicals found in tobacco smoke have had an effect on your taste buds. You will notice that when you quit smoking, food will begin to taste better. So in reality, the taste of tobacco is not pleasurable to our taste buds; tobacco tastes bad because it is a bitter plant. The extreme heat in one's mouth from the inhalation of tobacco smoke destroys your taste buds and diminishes your acuity to taste over time. Tobacco has destroyed your taste buds, so you don't even realize how horrible it and its four thousand-plus chemicals taste. Tobacco has a hold on you. Don't be a victim.

2. Smoking gives me something to do with my hands.

Some people say they enjoy smoking because it gives them something to do with their hands, or that they believe they are orally fixated. If this was the case, then one would not need to light the cigarette to satisfy this fixation or neurosis. If you need something to do with your hands, then just hold the cigarette in your hand and don't light it. The same applies to oral fixation. When you feel your need for something in your mouth, buy plastic cigarettes and put one between your lips and suck on it. Remember, you smoke because you are addicted to nicotine, not because you are orally fixated or need to do something with your hands. You can substitute the cigarette with a sugar-free lollipop or mint. This will solve your need to have something in your mouth. Using these statements as reasons why you can't quit is utter nonsense. Stop lying to yourself, using excuses why you continue to smoke!

3. Boredom.

Some offer the explanation that smoking makes time go by faster and helps with boredom. This is a sorry excuse. Boredom is a state of mind. If this is one of your excuses, then you need to reevaluate your life and find more positive things to revitalize it, such as making new friends, finding new hobbies, or practicing meditation or prayer. If you are shy and find it difficult meeting friends, either buy a new computer or use the old one you have and get online and meet some new people to deal with your boredom. Use my Web site at the end of the book for the links to quit-smoking groups and other links you can join to meet new friends. Yoga and exercise are just a few examples of good substitutes for your addiction if you use smoking to combat boredom.

The cigarette is not your friend! It is your worst enemy and is also the enemy of all within its poison-laden smoke. Cigarettes will rob you, your family, and your friends of good health.

You gain absolutely nothing positive from smoking. When you quit, you have to realize that the emotions you had vis-à-vis smoking, giving you comfort, were all in your head. It was the nicotine, increasing your brain chemistry to a heightened level, which was abnormal. Do you think it is natural to be addictive to a substance? Free your addiction by knowledge and start using your head. Smoking does nothing for you. Understand and accept this. You gain nothing from smoking, and it only harms your body. Why pay hundreds, and thousands, and tens of thousands of dollars for something that harms you? Does that make any sense?

CHAPTER 20

Common Sense

The addiction factor in relation to smoking is not fully understood. It could be a gene. It could be the power of suggestion through media representation. It could be a variety of factors. We are not sure exactly what causes some people to smoke, and others to hate everything about smoking. Why is it logical to some that smoking is dangerous, and others just don't care that smoking has the power to kill more people in America than heroine, crack, marijuana, cocaine, alcohol, AIDS, car accidents, murder, and fire combined? All the health conditions associated with smoking are preventable. All you do is quit. Some people only smoke one or two cigarettes a day, while others smoke a pack or more. It doesn't matter how much you smoke. Smoking kills and destroys your system every time you smoke.

This is a strong statement, and you may choose to ignore or deny the statistics. That's okay. Being skeptical is not always a bad thing. You should not believe everything you read. I, and most researchers, would admit you can find supporting data to prove or disapprove almost anything. This is, however, not a book about the evidence and proof with the supporting statistics to prove how bad smoking is for you. Instead, it is a book about becoming in tune with your common sense and your inner self, to help you better understand your addictions, so you can successfully become a nonsmoker for the rest of your life. It is as simple as that. We all know inherently what is good for our body and what is harmful. All the creatures in the universe know this. A bird knows to eat only berries from nonpoisonous trees, and if by chance it chooses one that does not agree with its system, it will not eat from that tree again.

Your first memory from your first cigarette should have been enough to have made you avoid cigarettes. This is why I believe there have to be other reasons behind why we choose to smoke, although we absolutely know that smoking is not healthy. When I took a drag from my first cigarette, I knew that cigarettes were bad for me. I coughed and coughed, I felt faint, and I wanted to throw up after just a few puffs.

We as humans often don't listen to our innermost feelings. The simplest of organisms, such as amoeba, would move away from cigarette smoke if blown into its path. We possess higher intelligence, yet we sometimes forget or choose to ignore what is just good old common sense. You already know that cigarettes are not good for you. You also know how important it is to exercise and eat a balanced diet. We all know, as intelligent beings, that we should stimulate our minds more with higher learning, read more, and watch less television. We just don't listen anymore and choose instead to ignore.

Always choose truth in your life and gear yourself toward what is positive. It is okay to accept that you are having trouble with quitting and are addicted. An addiction helps one cope through difficult times. I spoke earlier about my weight problem and how I gained more than eighty pounds in three years. The answer was simple; I was employed in a job I hated. My relationship with my girlfriend was failing. My future did not look bright. I felt empty and I ate. Smoking filled a temporary void in my life. The problem with addictions is, they do not heal or fix or solve the problem. So even if you do not believe the research and statistics relating to smoking and your health, then believe in Murphy's Law, which states: What you least expect to happen, can and will. Choose health over illness. Every organ and cell in your body will benefit from you not smoking. By smoking, you are depriving your cells of a vital nutrient—oxygen. The carbon monoxide in tobacco smoke competes with the oxygen in our body. Smoking also robs your brain of vital oxygen. A mind is a terrible thing to waste. Don't smoke.

CHAPTER 21
The Casual Smoker

Even if you are a person who smokes only socially, it is still too much. The casual smoker is more fortunate than those who smoke twenty to sixty cigarettes a day. If you are such a smoker, quit now. Chances are that you too, may one day become addicted, and your one-cigarette-a-week habit will become a-pack-a-day habit. Before you know it, you are smoking more than two packs a day.

Smoking is *not* attractive, and by smoking socially, you put yourself at a disadvantage. Many nonsmokers tend to see smokers as weak, out-of-control people. Most women and men I know say that they would never date a smoker, since smokers tend to have bad breath, yellow teeth, low stamina, and low self-esteem. How can you care about yourself and smoke? If you don't take care of yourself, how is it possible to care and love another person?

Smoking is addictive, and it is a habit you are likely not aware of, it's just a habit. Just think for a minute how many puffs you take in a day. The typical smoker takes about eight to twelve puffs from a cigarette. Under normal conditions, one will not require another puff until the nicotine blood level has diminished—usually a little less than ninety minutes. The craving begins again, and one takes another eight to twelve puffs of another cigarette, and so on, and so on. This cycle continues for the rest of one's life, unless one escapes the nicotine habit by quitting. It is something you do unconsciously. Do the math about how many puffs of cigarettes you inhale in a day.

Assignment # 2: Realizing your habit.

For this assignment, it will be necessary to carry a pen and paper with you for two days, or until you finish a full pack of cigarettes so you can analyze your smoking patterns.

1. I want you to count how many puffs out of your total amount of cigarettes you take. Remember, the assignments in this book are not negotiable. Please take the time to do them. Don't be stubborn or too smart for your own good. I want you to also record the times and the activity just before you light up that cigarette. Is it just as the phone rings? Before you begin eating? After your meal? Every time you walk outside? Every time you get into your car? Every time you take a break at work?
2. Notice your patterns and record them for two days. When you smoke, write down the time and the number of puffs you inhaled for each cigarette. Gaining insight into your habit is crucial. This is your habit, and ignorance of your addiction will only take you further into denial.
3. Do you see a pattern, or do you light up whenever you can, wherever it is allowed? Please don't read any further until you have recorded this information for forty-eight hours. Maybe buy a small pocket notebook to jot down your patterns.
4. After you have done this, continue reading from this point.

So … close the book now and begin reading two days from now. If you are not a smoker and have quit smoking already, take a day to observe others smoke. Notice how they smoke. Visualize how each breath of tobacco smoke they inhale enters their lungs and body. Notice how unattractive smoking is. Notice the horrible smell.

.

.

.

How did you do? Did you actually do the assignment? I hope so!

The power of tobacco products comes from nicotine levels in the blood. Did you notice you needed a quick fix approximately every forty to ninety minutes? I noticed this mostly when I was around people or within an environment that allowed me to smoke. Why could I travel from New York to Nepal and not have one cigarette? It was because I was not allowed to smoke on the plane. Why is it so difficult when I am at home or outside, not to smoke? Because the need to smoke is all in the mind. Many chain smokers can put their urge on hold in movies theaters or at a shopping mall or airplane for hours on end, but immediately after, they rush for that quick fix.

When nicotine blood levels get low from abstention, one craves another cigarette. This nagging urge continues until one lights up another butt. Sadly enough, some people smoke until they die. Please wake up and think about all the lies that you have learned about smoking and begin analyzing your addiction so you can take hold of it.

Ask yourself: Do I want to get sick? Do I want to be controlled by cigarettes? Do I want to cause harm through secondhand smoke to others? Do I even care? You do not have to believe that secondhand smoke is dangerous for it to harm others. It is harmful whether you accept it or not. It goes deeper than why you let substances or other people control you. Self-esteem is usually the root. You cannot love yourself and simultaneously cause yourself harm. By having compassion yourself, you will quit hurting yourself, and you will decide to rise above destructive behavior, not only for you own benefit, but also for the benefit of your friends and family, and those you choose to smoke around.

No substance has the ability to take away the stress in your life or help you cope better. Alcohol, illegal drugs, prescription drugs, chocolate, food, sex, money, shopping, and other addictive substances, offer no real relief. They may offer some relief temporarily, but they don't get to the root of the problem.

You are your emotions, and you are your happiness. Cigarettes, alcohol, and drugs destroy your nerves and negatively affect your mind. I can't tell you why you smoke. You need to discover this for yourself. If you want to quit just simply tell yourself you have had enough and go for it!

I made this choice in Nepal when I threw my pack of cigarettes out the window. At that point in my life, I was not happy and felt like a loser. I was at an age where I believed a man should be established and settled with a wife, a child, and a condominium. I should have been successful but was not. I smoked to comfort myself. The more insecure I felt with my life, the more I smoked. But when I actually looked at the things I had accomplished, it wasn't that I was a loser, nor was it that dismal. I looked at my life and realized that I had done a lot. I have traveled to Egypt, Nepal, Tibet, Germany, France, and England. I have also traveled extensively within the United States. I have excellent friends all around the world, I have a great family, and I am healthy. I really had nothing to complain about. I was searching for happiness, which was already part of me.

I had made some mistakes in my life, but all the choices I've made, bad or good, have given me knowledge. I bought things and traveled to escape my insecurities. I thought buying new clothes and spending money would make me happy. It did at times, and I had great moments. I now know that happiness begins within. Nothing—no man, no women, no child, no friend, not even a cigarette—can make you happy or relieve your stress. Stress can be relieved by calming down, using relaxation techniques and exercising—not by smoking a cigarette. If you truly have a lot of stress in your life, plan an appointment with your physician to discuss possible choices to relieve stress.

People have moved to different cities, changed jobs, only to find they are still depressed and unhappy. I accept that I did not save or invest my money wisely, to settle down with a woman—and to date, I have no children. When I was twenty, I planned to be married with one kid by the age of thirty. But why focus on the negative and what I did not accomplish? Instead, I have changed my mindset, and decided that if I want these things in my life, I must work hard to get them. As I get older, I realize that everything worthwhile takes time, patience, and hard work. So instead, I focus now on the good and learn from the bad or the painful. I also have learned to focus on the here and now. If I'm washing the dishes, I focus on washing the dishes, not on my job, my girlfriend, or anything else. It is all about being mindful of your thoughts, actions, and tasks.

It must be the same thing when quitting smoking. When I give you the cue to stop smoking, you must give 100 percent to quit. While you are reading this book, you need to focus on quitting: a plan, a schedule, a preparation for the section in this book that you will stop smoking. Staying mindful is very important. It would be a waste of your time if you are reading this book and your mind is somewhere else, or if you are reading this book and ignoring all the assignments or instructions.

Commit to focusing and staying in the moment. Take control over your thoughts. When you find a section, word, or sentence in this book that does not sit well with you, absorb it and move on. Focus not on what is negative or what seems incorrect, but instead focus on you becoming a nonsmoker. This is what being mindful is about. Realizing your reactive mind, accepting it, and going back to what is important is what this book is about.

It is now evident that the path I chose was necessary for me to grow and learn. I realized all the money in the world, being married, and raising children in my own condo would have not made me happy and might have led to divorce, bankruptcy, and a broken home. I could not feel satisfied no matter what I did. I had to be content with what I had and stop judging the things in my life I did not accomplish, focusing instead on those I had achieved.

When I stopped judging others and myself and started to live in the present, all seemed to fall into place. This will also happen to you. One of the things that helped me stay clean from cigarettes was clearing my mind with controlled thought, which is known as meditation.

I will teach you some basic techniques on relaxation, how to calm your mind. When your mind is constantly active, no growth can happen. You mind needs a dormant period to rebuild and grow. Before learning to meditate, my mind was always active. I thought about everything. I worried, even in my sleep, and I had nightmares. Meditation is nothing more than conscious sleeping. There is nothing mystic or religious about meditation. Meditation is simply used to condition and strengthen your brain. I realize that you may be saying you bought this book to learn how to quit smoking, not to learn about spirituality, meditation, going inward, etc. You've come this far. Just hang in there and be open-minded.

CHAPTER 22
Calming Your Mind through Meditation

Meditation is easy and simple, and is nothing more than conscious, controlled relaxation. It is not only for the highly spiritual or for those involved in the "New Age" movement. This is a misconception. One does not have to be spiritual to meditate. Instead one gains self-awareness and spirituality through meditation. Meditation is nothing more than giving your conscious mind a break from stress, and it will help you become aware of your thoughts and give you added insights into yourself. As you continue to meditate your life will become less complex and chaotic, and instead will become simple, ordered, and beautiful. Meditation silences the mind and causes you to become more aware without having to analyze every situation. Negative emotions also seem to dissipate with continued, deeper meditation. When you quiet the mind via meditation, all of your senses become heightened. You will tend to notice the small things in your life.

This may all seem a bit hard to believe at first, but it is true. Meditation can accomplish miraculous things to one's soul and help one better deal with life and its surprises. Meditation is concentration in its simplest form. It is thought without the emotional past attached.

The need for a cigarette is merely thought. You have the choice to control it by either giving into it or changing it into a repulsion. Through meditation, you will gain control over your thoughts.

This will be your greatest challenge. Quitting cold turkey was one of the most difficult experiences of my life. Of course, I faced many other challenges in my life that were difficult, but none had lasted as long as quitting smoking had. I wanted to prove to myself that I was stronger than my thoughts.

I am now in control of my life; I'm not controlled by an ad campaign that persuaded me when I was a child that smoking was cool and I was cool because I smoked. The only way to gain back control was to reject all attachments to tobacco products. Meditation was the tool that allowed me to become aware of my thoughts in order to control them. I am happy to say I no longer enjoy cigarettes. I hate them and I don't want them in my life, and I will no longer allow them to cause me harm. I won't allow smoking in my home or car. I can now truly say I hate tobacco.

In order for you to remain a nonsmoker, you must also develop a hatred toward tobacco. You have to stop believing the hype about cigarettes and start accepting the fact that smoking kills and does absolutely nothing positive for you. Meditation is one way for you to start accepting what you actually already know. Meditation enables you to capture the something within you that is peaceful, calm, rejuvenating, significant, and all knowing. The calming of the mind through meditation helps build self-esteem and character to combat your addictions, fears, and denials. This in turn will help you to never smoke again. Meditation is not only for the spiritual and those who believe in it. There is no religion attached to it, as it exists in almost every religion—Islam, Catholicism, Judaism, Buddhism, Hinduism, and Taoism—and in religious practices from the Americas to Africa.

Meditation is as simple as clearing your mind and witnessing your reality without judgment, fear, guilt, or regret. It is an active form of relaxation and begins by fully concentrating on a thought, sound, or substance. It then transcends to another realm, which becomes more passive and automatic. Meditation will take you beyond your thoughts.

I will help you learn the simple techniques necessary to start you on the road to quitting your nasty habit. However, you will need to commit at least five minutes a day three times a week to set aside to quiet your mind. This is all you need to agree on right now. Going inward is an essential element to successfully quitting. Don't be afraid of meditation. Don't panic! Meditation can be as simple as lying in bed and concentrating just before you fall asleep at night, or just before you awake in the morning.

Later, if you choose to become more involved, you can learn other techniques from the masters and gurus. I want you to feel comfortable. I will give you some guidelines, but how you choose to meditate will be entirely up to you.

CHAPTER 23

Techniques to Meditate

There are many ways to meditate, but there is really no perfect or incorrect way to do it. Meditation leads you to a better understanding into the self. The mind/body connection is a powerful tool. Meditation has the power to remove toxins from your body, improve your concentration, lower blood pressure, improve your health, and create a more positive you. Just taking time to relax your mind and give it some relief from daily stress will benefit you more than you can imagine. The main reason it is so important is that it releases the constant sensory input that bombards our minds every minute of every day. Here are some simple guidelines to meditation:

1) Meditation is best if done every day. The more you meditate, the better it will be for you.

2) Meditation should be practiced in a quiet place.

3) Meditation should be done seated with the spine erect.

4) Meditation should not be done after a meal. One should wait at least one hour after eating.

Basically, that is all there is to it. First, you need to choose a place at home where you won't be distracted for at least five minutes. Music can also be used when silence in the home is not possible, or when one finds it difficult to quiet the mind. When I first began meditating, I found it very difficult to quiet my mind, for my mind would wander. I enjoyed listening to classical music from the baroque period; two of my favorite composers are Handel and Bach. You may prefer sounds of the ocean or rain forest. One important factor of music for meditation is that the tempo must be slow, around sixty beats per minute.

Some research done in Russia suggests that music with a tempo of sixty beats or less is beneficial to enhanced learning and mind reprogramming … the point being that the music you choose for meditation should be no faster than your resting pulse; generally this can range from seventy-one to eighty-six beats per minute. You should have no problem finding meditation music for this assignment. Just go to a popular music store or visit the link section of my Web site for reference.

After your mind becomes quiet, then you can focus on meditating without music. Remember, the assignments in this book are not an option. Quieting the mind is necessary for you to successfully quit smoking. Don't freak out about the word "meditation." It can be as easy as lying on your bed and focusing your thoughts for five minutes. There are no difficult assignments in this book and none that require much energy. Meditation begins with concentration. One can choose to focus on an object such as an apple, a flower, or even a mountain. Many choose to concentrate on their breathing or a repetitive sound known as a mantra, while others may prefer a controlled thought or visualization. Okay, now it is time to take out a pen and paper and take some notes, so you can write down the techniques to meditate.

Posture

The correct posture for meditation is sitting with your spine, neck, and head erect. Your hands are in your lap. When sitting in a chair, it is best to lean forward slightly, so that the chair does not support your back. If this is difficult for you, then just lean back. I want you to feel comfortable. If this is still uncomfortable at first, you can always do it lying down on the floor or in your bed with your legs uncrossed. There are no hard-core rules to meditation. The important thing is to make time to meditate. I don't want you to feel as if this is a burden. I want you to enjoy it. Please give it a try!

Breathing

With your eyes closed, feeling comfortable, and in your chosen meditation position, breathe in deeply and let out a huge, big sigh. Do this twice more. This will tell your brain that meditation is about to begin. Now focus on your natural breathing. Don't try to control it, simply notice your breath. Notice it as you breathe in through your nostrils. Is one nostril more open than the other? Doesn't matter! Just witness, don't judge. Leave all judgment out of your meditation. Now breathe out slowly through your mouth. Notice your natural breath at first. Notice your breathing rhythm. Is your inhalation longer than your exhalation? Is your breathing heavy or is it smooth? Remember, only witness, don't question! Another important factor is when your mind begins to wander, don't force it back. Just realize you got off track and go back to concentrating on your breath.

1. Now try to breathe in slowly for a count of six.
2. Hold your breath for a count of three.
3. Exhale for a count of eight. Breathe slowly and smoothly.
4. Do this four more times. This is a great way to relax. You can even do it on your morning commute if you take public transportation.
5. Concentrate on the rate of your breathing, so that inhalations and exhalations are even and smooth. Now at first, this may be difficult for you to do. If so, you can adapt the rate or time of your controlled breathing.
6. Now go back and breathe naturally. Notice the airflow through your nose as you inhale, and visualize it coming from

your lungs to your nasal cavity and back out through your mouth.

7. Now breathe in silently using your normal breath as you tell yourself, "I am bringing in oxygen to nourish my mind, body and spirit." Visualize oxygen and nutrients going through your nose and whole body as you inhale.

   As you exhale, envision all the impurities, such as the toxins from tobacco smoke, leaving your body through your mouth. Tell yourself you are releasing all impurities and negative energies into the air and visualize these toxins leaving your lungs and being destroyed as they come in contact with the air.

   Tell yourself that you are a nonsmoker and that smoking makes you sick. Tell yourself that you choose health instead of illness. Do all of this with your eyes closed.

   Don't worry about your mind moving on to other thoughts, just let it go and bring it back. Never force it to stay focused, because the more you try, the more it will refuse. You will lose concentration and your mind will wander off.

8. Just relax and mellow out. Now continue breathing in for a count of eight, hold for four, and out for ten. Do this twice and now just visualize yourself as a nonsmoker. Visualize someone asking you for a cigarette and you say "No, I don't smoke." Visualize in your mind's eye all the actions or situations that usually give you the urge to smoke, such as a stressful event, when outside, after eating, or drinking coffee or alcohol, etc., and with each visualization or thought, I want you to cancel out the emotion with a big X in your mind. See the X and cross out each emotion, thought, word, or feeling that usually makes you want to smoke, and say in your mind "cancel." After you have finished, just let your mind wander for two minutes. Don't judge or analyze what pops up into your mind, but instead witness it. Now slowly count to ten and wake up.

In about a week or more, you will begin to feel comfortable with the silence, and it will become natural. Remember, the mind does not like chance, so your mind will attempt to control your thoughts, in order for you to stop the meditation or make excuses why this is a silly exercise. Ignore your thoughts and do it anyway. You have control. It is easy to remain stagnant and do the same old thing while trying new things. This takes no power at all! However, to go against the thought and to choose action instead, takes control. Hopefully, you will start to meditate and take time out to do it every day. If you can't do it every day, make a contract with yourself to do it at least three times a week.

Now take out your notebook or a piece of paper, so you can schedule which days and what time you will meditate. This is your private time. Silence your phone and answering machine; close your door; and if you live with other people, tell them to not disturb you for at least ten minutes. Remember, you are in control of your meditation and of your thoughts. Train your mind as an athlete would train his body. Go beyond the norm. You can also do this on your commute if you take public transportation.

Stop reading here and practice your breathing techniques for a few days. I also want to think about some of the things that I spoke about in this book while you meditate. Please close the book now and resume reading after you have done at least two days of meditation. See you then …

Advanced Meditation

After you feel comfortable with the breathing exercises, you are ready to focus on an object. You can choose anything to focus on, but I would suggest that to begin with, you chose something, an object, that has little meaning to you. This will help you focus better—an apple, a lemon, a chair, perhaps a tree. When focusing on the object, notice it as if you're seeing it for the first time; visualize it in your mind's eye, but don't approach it with rational thought. Just see it.

For instance, if you choose an apple to meditate on, visualize its color, its shape; does it have a twig, with a leaf attached? How many notches are on the bottom of the apple? Be curious, not smart. Do not try to define, judge, or understand it. Don't label it. Just observe it as an infant would through its eyes. Infants have no preconceived notions or judgment. This is exactly what I want you to do, to see the object and experience it without attaching any emotion to it. Don't worry about your mind wandering. Just let it wander and then refocus.

There is no "failing" with meditation—no right or wrong, just degree of clarity. Your mind will jump from subject to subject, but you will also learn how to refocus it without energy or emotion. Just visualize your drifting thoughts as clouds passing in the sky. See them go by and fade away. Every controlled refocus brings you closer to success. You may at times feel as if you are getting nowhere, and nothing is coming out of this practice. This is normal. Nothing will come out of it if you force it or expect it.

Meditation is first and foremost a controlled state of passive awareness. If you attempt to find rewards for the practice, you will be disappointed. Meditation will change you radically, but determining it to change you will only slow down the process. Just let it flow. Even if you feel you are not benefiting from it, you are.

This may seem a bit strange at first. Feeling confused, feeling nothing, is good. After a while, you will begin to understand the power of meditation and notice that life around you will seem different. You will begin to be conscious of your actions, emotions, and feelings before they have the ability to get you upset. You will also not "sweat the small stuff" as you may have done in the past. Your mind will be calmed and things won't irritate you as they once did. There will be a significant inner transformation and enlightenment of your mind, body, and spirit. It happens automatically. This is not to say that you won't get upset, or that meditation will cure all of your stressful events, because it won't. Meditation will just help you be more aware and focused—of yourself and what's happening around you.

There are many degrees of meditation; the one presented to you in this book is structured to assist you with relaxation and going inward.

After you do your visualizations and breathing techniques at the beginning of your meditation, you can then focus on your body as a whole. Begin to notice your whole body, from your toenails on your feet, up to the hair on your head. Notice how your legs feel, your arms, your eyebrows, your fingers. Examine the tension within your body and release it through exhalation. Now as you observe your body, notice how it feels, but remember not to judge what you are feeling. Good things may pop in your mind, along with bad memories and things that happened throughout your day. Just let them flow. Don't hold on to the thoughts. Give the visualization, or the lack of it, no thought or energy. Just be aware.

Next, you can begin to focus on a thought, a word, a positive phrase ... and alternate between visualization and breathing. There are many wonderful books and audiotapes that can help assist you with other techniques of meditation.

CHAPTER 24

Be Aware of What You Are Doing

It is very important to monitor your thoughts. Many people are unaware of their conscious thoughts and the messages they send. These messages have the power to change your life. Every time you smoke when you feel nervous, your mind gets the message that smoking has the ability to calm your nerves. You are the programmer to your mindset. If you send your brain positive messages about cigarettes and smoking, your brain will believe them to be true, and you will stay hooked to a habit. Analyze and be conscious of what you are doing and of the reasons behind what you are doing. From now on, I want you to be conscious of your smoking.

1) Realize the consequences of your addiction.

2) Realize what you are doing to your body.

3) Realize when you tend to smoke more.

4) Don't analyze or judge your observations. Just be aware.

5) Notice what actions increase your cravings to smoke.

6) Be honest with yourself.

7) Get out of denial.

8) Be aware that you are actually paying the tobacco companies to cause you harm. Realize you are foolishly jeopardizing your

health and welfare by your addictions to nicotine. Smoking is robbing you of good health.

I am not trying to scare you. I am just being up front with you and saying if you continue to smoke, you will have a very good chance of experiencing one or more of the following illnesses and conditions: heart attacks, bronchitis, cancer, or stroke. Smoking is not okay and it does absolutely nothing for you. Start feeding your thoughts on these notions. Every time you smoke out of habit, such as after dinner, or when outside, or in your home, realize that you are causing each cell in your body harm. If you continue to feed yourself bad input about smoking, your brain will get the message that smoking is truly harmful, and your cravings will diminish.

Hopefully, some of this is sinking in. Smokers can be the toughest addicts to convince that their habits have huge consequences. They hear the warnings, but they go in one ear and out the other.

Please don't allow yourself to be stubborn and bullheaded with the messages that I am giving you. Please don't ignore what you feel inside. Do something about it! You have the power and the ability to stop! Why on earth are you paying the cigarette companies your hard-earned money to cause you harm? I speak with great concern about your health, and I speak to you from knowledge. Everything that you do in life has consequences. Ignoring is part of your addiction, and nicotine is also causing you to think irrationally. Take care of yourself and don't let your urges take control over what is logical!

A major portion of the first edition of this book was written at the bedside of my beautiful mother, Eris, who was hospitalized after a heart attack and two strokes within a two-week period. She now has no short-term memory and has to relearn how to do all the things that came naturally before, like walking, talking, reading, writing, and taking care of herself.

My mother lived life as she wanted, ignoring the doctors and their regimen for eating right and exercising. She did not care about what she ate or about exercise or taking medication to regulate her high blood pressure. She loved fried foods and foodstuff that she knew would one day destroy her. I have often gotten angry at her rebellious nature to do what she wanted and when she wanted, choosing to ignore what she knew was logical. This stubbornness and lack of respect for herself about exercising and eating right caused her to lose so much. I wish she wasn't so stubborn. Sometimes stubbornness keeps you from learning from your mistakes, and the consequence may be having to repeat them.

Two months after my mother came home from rehabilitation, she fell and broke her hip. I was, along with a live-in assistant, taking care of her. This could have been prevented, had she listened to her physical therapist's instructions about using her walker while at home. She was too proud to use her walker and felt that she did not need it, and preferred to walk proudly on her own two feet. Her disregard has caused her to be bound to a wheelchair for life.

After her fall, she had another stroke and now is totally dependent on other people for all of her needs. Her doctors warned her about her high cholesterol, poor eating habits, and the importance of exercise. She did not care, nor did she listen. I love my mother so much, and to see her in so much pain, with her inability to speak, has caused me great sorrow and depression that I thought I would never get over. Two years later, my mother is on a respirator, tube-fed, can't move, and has had her leg amputated because of diabetes. My family and I are praying that God will take her any day now. We have been praying for a year. She is in so much pain and she can't speak to express her needs.

I am now writing the second edition of this book, at her bedside, and praying for God to relieve her of her pain … and as I'm writing this, tears are falling from my face. My mother worked in a hospital as a nurse. She knew about health, exercise, and eating right, but she chose to ignore what was logical. Her consequences were really harsh.

If you continue to smoke, it will have an effect upon you and all your loved ones. The suffering caused by addiction is always a shared experience, affecting family and friends, harming the very people you care the most about.

Please don't tell me about how you know someone who lived to be 90, who smoked and drank all his life. There are always exceptions and you are probably not one of the exceptions. You are what you put into your body. If you sit all day, eat what you want, smoke and drink, and never exercise—life will reward you with illness.

Don't allow yourself to be destroyed by an addiction. Your body can only take so much damage and will then break down. Then you, your family, and your friends will feel the pain of your neglect, denial, and stubbornness. If you continue to smoke, you will *without a doubt* fall prey to a smoking-related disease of some sort. Quitting will be difficult the first month, but in the long run, it will definitely be easier to handle than having cancer, a heart attack, diabetes, or a stroke.

The human body is strong and durable and can cope with a good amount of abuse and wear and tear, but the body can only take so much abuse before breaking down. I give you these warnings, along with the message for you to stop your habit before it is too late!

According to the Center of Disease Control and Prevention, men who smoke increase their risk of death from lung cancer by more than twenty-two times, and from bronchitis and emphysema by nearly ten times. Women who smoke increase their risk of dying from lung cancer by nearly twelve times, and the risk of dying from bronchitis and emphysema by more than ten times. Smoking *triples* the risk of dying from heart disease among middle-aged men and women.

You need to seriously think about quitting, now and forever. It is not too late. Your body can rejuvenate itself and do incredible things if you just stop abusing it.

In a little more than a couple of months, your overall energy will rise and your lungs will increase their effectiveness in clearing mucus and fighting off infection and will start repairing themselves. That's the miracle of the human body: Stop the damage and the repair mechanism kicks in. After the first year of being a nonsmoker, your risk of heart disease is halved in comparison with a smoker's. When you stop smoking, your lungs will begin to clear themselves. You will cough up all kinds of horrible-looking phlegm in your morning shower; this is a good thing.

After ten years you will have significantly reduced your chances of cancer of the mouth, throat, esophagus, lungs, kidneys, bladder, and pancreas, as well as strokes. It will be as if you never smoked. Quitting smoking is one of the most intelligent things you can do for yourself, along with exercise and eating right. There are many excellent books about good diet, so I won't expand on that subject. Exercising can be as simple as walking just fifteen or twenty minutes a day to begin with.

Practice your meditation assignment for a couple of days before you begin reading the next chapter. Get your pen and paper and take notes on the procedure instructed above. I know that it may be unusual for you to be told when to read and when not to, but remember this book is not about going with the norm. It is about thinking outside of the box. I understand that you may want to read on and continue, but please just follow my suggestion. It is very important that you take a rest from the book and meditate on thoughts felt, visualizations, and breathing techniques. The mind needs time to absorb some of the concepts presented to you here. This book will work on both a conscious and subconscious level simultaneously. This is why it is important to take a rest from reading. While resting or sleeping, your brain will go over all the material you've taken in so far, and this will optimize your learning.

Please close the book and come back after you have meditated for two days.

CHAPTER 25

Will You Gain Weight When You Quit Smoking?

Why is it easier for some people to quit smoking than others? Mind control.

I have read scientific journals about addictive genes, which play a role as to why smokers and alcoholics find it so difficult to kick their habit. Don't short change yourself. If you want to quit, you will quit. It is very easy to say that you are addicted to cigarettes. Do something about it! Will you gain weight if you quit smoking? Yeah, you probably will. Some research shows that nicotine suppresses the appetite by causing the liver to release glycogen, so there may be some evidence that even if you eat the same amount of food as you did when you smoked, you *may* gain some extra pounds. If you know you will gain weight, then just eat less, exercise more, and watch your calories and fat intake.

I did not gain a pound when I quit smoking. I *lost* a considerable amount of weight after quitting smoking. Don't just think about joining a health spa, do it. If you can't afford to, then cut down on the carbs and exercise. We already talked about the 24/7 fitness clubs that offer plenty of time. Rent/buy a video exercise tape or exercise book. Just do some form of exercise. When you are in continuous motion for more than twenty minutes, it becomes beneficial. There are many ways to exercise for free. Bike, jog, hike, climb. Walk! All the expensive weights and equipment in the world cannot match the value of walking as an exercise. Try at least ten to twenty minutes per day, work up to forty-five, and then an hour, and continue walking every day for the rest of your life. Instead of driving short distances, try walking. Get off a stop or two earlier from the train, bus, or taxi and walk the rest of the way to your destination. Swing your arms and get a pace going; swing your hips if you feel like it, you'll inspire other people to do it too.

Can't get started? Don't get distracted by your own excuses. Don't procrastinate! Excuses don't apply here. What I am saying is that it doesn't matter if you believe you are orally fixated to have a cigarette in your mouth, or if you have a gene that predisposes you to smoking, or if you have an addictive personality.

One great thing that separates humans from animals is that humans can alter their destiny with thought and do not have to act on their instincts or feelings. We are able to control our thoughts and desires. After you quit, you should schedule an appointment with your physician to talk about exercise plans and vitamins and herbal supplements to help cleanse your body. There are many herbal/vitamin formulas for cleansing. Get advice from a health professional. Some vitamins and herbal products can have some reactions when taken with prescribed medications.

On average, smokers gain an extra ten to twenty pounds after quitting smoking; that takes in a lot of territory, from zero weight gain to several pounds. Although quitting smoking reduces your chances of many diseases, it is associated with marked weight gain and presumably insulin resistance. Nicotine suppresses the appetite, and it is believed that it causes the liver to release glycogen, which raises your blood sugar. Thus when you quit, you may have increased hunger sensation. Some researchers believe that nicotine may block a pathway in carbohydrate storage pathways; others believe there is an unknown substance within tobacco that controls weight. This would account for the added weight that many experience when they quit smoking, even when their diets have not changed.

When you quit, expect to have a craving for carbohydrates and sweets. Now … if you have been carefully following the book, you know that concentrating on a possible weight gain is not going to help you quit. It will be a barrier if you choose to focus on weight gain. Instead, know that there is a possibility for weight gain because of carbohydrates—eat less bread, pasta, cakes, and ice cream. When quitting smoking, it is necessary to cleanse your system. Here is a list of things to include in your diet:

1. Eat plenty of fruits, nuts, and vegetables. Broccoli is rich in the plant nutrient isothiocyanate, which seems to help detoxify cigarette smoke in the lungs of smokers. For nuts, include sunflower and flaxseeds. They supply omega three and omega six fats to help keep the linings of the lung healthy as well as the brain. Please also discuss any suggestions recommended here with your physician, since not only herbs and vitamins can have drug interactions with your current prescribed medication, so can foodstuffs.

2. Eat vitamin C- and E-enriched foods. Good sources of vitamin C are kiwi fruits, melons, oranges, red peppers, broccoli, kale, strawberries, dark green vegetables, and wheat germ. They help to protect the cells in your body from potentially damaging free radicals caused from smoking. And smoking reduces the vitamin C in your body.

3. Use fresh garlic cloves in food preparation, or eat it raw. While garlic is gathering a reputation for helping to maintain a healthy heart, regular amounts of garlic seem to also help the body fight off infections. This is especially important when you are quitting smoking. It has been shown that garlic can protect us from various pollutants and heavy metals. Using garlic after quitting can help rid your body of some of the excess toxins.

4. Chlorella is believed to be a powerful detoxification aid for heavy metals and other toxic substances. Chlorella tabs or powder can be found at most health food stores.

5. Eat more fiber. It helps promote friendly bacteria in your gut, therefore helping to fight digestive infection.

6. Try aloe vera juice, which can be bought at most health stores. Other great juices are bilberry, cranberry, papaya, and blueberry. Vegetable juicing may be one of the keys to good health as it is an important source of raw food. Each of us needs raw foods every day, and juicing is an excellent technique to assure you receive large quantities of such raw foods.

7. Eat plenty of probiotic yogurt with live cultures.

8. Drink plenty of water, no less than a quart a day.

9. Increase your protein consumption of oily fish, such as salmon and tuna, quinoa, tofu, and seafood.

10. Prepare for the withdrawal symptoms that come along with quitting smoking. Support from your family, friends, coworkers, and your doctor is also essential. Tell them that you have decided to quit smoking with this book, and that you will appreciate their help. Also try to avoid friends or coworkers who smoke and ask them not to smoke around you. Stay away from soda, coffee, and alcohol for at least two weeks. You don't need any extra triggers to spark your craving for nicotine.

Remember, once you quit, you can never have another cigarette. You will always be addicted to nicotine, thus you must stay away from it.

Exercise is extremely important after quitting smoking. It helps with stress, withdrawals symptoms, depression, hunger, and your spirit. It also helps your brain chemistry to deal with the lack of nicotine in your blood. Start slowly, consult with your medical doctor and do it. You can start with walking for fifteen minutes every other day. This is not difficult. Relaxation and meditation is also great in combination with exercise to soothe the mind and to recondition the spirit. If you are having difficulty with meditation alone, join a group or try yoga. The physical withdrawal symptoms will be gone in about a week. Meditation is essential to heal your spirit and your mind. So many people quit smoking but forget about healing the psyche. Meditation, exercise, and cleansing your body will help you with this. You must make an honest commitment to replace your negative behaviors and replace them with positive ones, such as meditation, exercising, and eating right.

CHAPTER 26
Willpower and Buddhist Thought

Traveling to Nepal taught me to be many things, but most important it taught me control and the theory of suffering. The Buddha discovered that the direct causes of suffering are desire or craving and ignorance. By developing wisdom, it destroys craving and ignorance, the two causes of addiction and suffering. Craving: people who desire to own things can never fully be satisfied. They crave all the latest fashions and technology toys and other things they see around them, like children in a toy shop. But like children too, they soon become dissatisfied with what they already have, and desire for more continues. Uncontrolled desires can also lead to addiction, as it does with smoking, drinking, and overeating; all lead to suffering and cause mental and physical harm. First it starts with one cigarette a day, then it turns to a pack a day habit. Nicotine becomes the craving; one becomes nervous, upset, and irritated when nicotine isn't in the blood for an hour. Because of desire and greed, people will lie, cheat, and steal to get their fix.

Ignorance is the inability to see the truth of things and see things as they really are, and this ignorance with smoking is tied to the craving. One stays in denial and lies to oneself because there is too much pain involved to quit the habit. Many people continue to smoke even after being diagnosed with cancer. Realize that we smoke not because we enjoy cigarettes and the four thousand-plus chemicals present, but because we are chemically addicted to nicotine. Why is America the fattest country? It is because of craving and ignorance. We want it fast and we want it supersized. We eat to satisfy our craving and eat till we feel stuffed, instead of eating to nourish our body.

Willpower is what I obtain from Buddhist thought: mental discipline. The Buddhists have an Eightfold Path to Enlightenment, which is purposely designed to get us from where we think we are to where we actually are.

1. Right view or understanding; this deals with selflessness and the impermanence of all things, which removes the roots of ignorance and enables us to see things as they truly are.

2. Right intention or motivation; we should try always to do what is right.

3. Right speech or communication; we should be truthful and kind in all we say. Speech is a powerful tool to influence others. When used wisely, many will benefit. Right speech includes the avoidance of: lying, spreading rumors, harsh speech, and idle chatter.

4. Right action or conduct; we should try to behave ourselves at all times. The practice of perfect action involves the respect for the life, property, and personal relationships of others. It helps to develop a character that is self-controlled and mindful of the rights of others.

5. Right vocation or livelihood; we should earn our living in a way which will not harm anyone.

6. Right effort; preventing unwholesome states of mind from arising. Facilitate good and wholesome states of mind. Bring to perfection wholesome mental states already present.

7. Right attention or mindfulness; be conscious of the functions of the body, sensations and feelings, mental activity, and spe-

cific ideas and thoughts. Meditation is key to achieving right mindfulness.

8. Right presence or concentration; this refers to the development of "mental muscle" to help one focus to accomplish the other goals of the eightfold path and will help you with remaining a nonsmoker.

Willpower is an extremely important task to control if you just stay in the present. It is unimportant how often you have failed in the past or attempted to quit a habit or addiction. What you do in the here and now is what matters.

Recalling your past mistakes or looking into your future will not bring you closer to becoming a nonsmoker. The key is to live in the present and be conscious of your past, without judging your past mistakes or events. The basic principle of the Eightfold Path to Enlightenment will help you stay focused. Combating past mistakes and failures brings a higher consciousness and greater inner strength. It feels good to conquer a past demon or to face it without judgment. Don't worry about a past event because it hinders you from becoming successful in the present. Be also aware of not pushing it under the rug as if it never existed. Recalling the past can be extremely positive if you witness it without guilt. This simply means recalling a difficult past feeling or memory, and viewing it without analyzing it or feeling emotional. This is called past remembrance without judgment. For some people it may be difficult, and it will take some time.

We as humans tend to judge others and ourselves. Judgment belongs only in the courthouse or in the afterlife. It is important to be aware of your past mistakes so you don't repeat them. It is not okay to believe you are your past. Learn from your mistakes and from those of others. Don't fear your past; if you do, it has the possibility to haunt you forever. We sometime forget we have control over our lives.

Failure used in a positive light can bring heightened success, if the realization of one's failure brings greater strength and spiritual growth to combat a difficult addiction. Feeling guilty about failure is an unnecessary emotion. The past is gone and it can't be changed. One cannot predict the future, so why use so much energy on things that we can't change or have no knowledge of? I know this may sound sweet on paper, but it is actually possible.

I have stopped worrying about everything and started living in the present and doing what I need to do to get things done. This is how I combated anxiety and depression from all that was going on in my life, what was destroying me along with my soul. I have quit smoking and do not worry about getting hooked on the habit again, because I choose to live in the present. I am aware of my feelings about cigarette smoke and tobacco use, and I choose health over illness, so I don't have to ponder about such insanity. I am a nonsmoker.

Devote your willpower to reaching one goal at a time. Scattering one's energies leaves things half-done. This is wasteful and limiting. Don't blame yourself for your past mistakes or feel guilty because you had such a difficult time quitting. Everyone fails and failure is not personal. Never accept failing as your faith. Your faith is to overcome your obstacles, not to be a prisoner to them.

My strength to quit came from honesty within and my newfound inner security. I spent a lot of money traveling to faraway lands to discover that the answers lie within. We have all heard about how important it is to go inward for happiness, and now you realize just how easy it is. The ability to quit has to come from within, not in the form of a pill, a patch, hypnotic tape, or even a book, unless one of these brings you to a greater understanding of yourself—as I hope you will gain from this book. There is absolutely nothing wrong with failure. So if you fail, just start again. You must understand this and tell yourself that there is nothing wrong with you. Quitting smoking can be difficult for most, but you have an advantage because you are reading this book to help you quit on every aspect possible: mind, body, and spirit.

CHAPTER 27
You are Blameless for Your Past

This is your key to successfully quitting smoking forever!

Assignment #3

Please take a few minutes to think about what you have read. Do you understand the message I have given you? Or are you just reading the words without much thought or concentration? Doing so won't help you much unless you apply it to your everyday life.

Here is an affirmation which will help you. I want you to repeat this to yourself until you truly believe it:

"I am not a prisoner of my past mistakes. I can't change yesterday, but I can start changing the present. I will become a nonsmoker and remain such forever. I don't enjoy smoking, and I don't want to smoke. Smoking is dangerous, and I choose health." Say this affirmation before each cigarette you smoke.

Your addiction to cigarettes is based on four things:

1. Your physical addiction to nicotine.
2. Your psychological addiction.
3. Rote habit.
4. Deprived soul.

Now, I am not trying to disrespect you, but I am telling you exactly what I see and what I have experienced in my own life. If you are still smoking with all you know about smoking in relationship to your health, there must be something more than the addiction. I want you to first start analyzing why you choose to remain hooked.

Take a minute or so to go over why you are still smoking. Is it because you enjoy smoking? You know this can't be true. The secret is that the desire to quit must come from realizing that you don't enjoy smoking, because smoking has no benefits. You need to realize all the disadvantages, such as jeopardizing your health, the health of others, and the cost.

Your success to quit will come when you stop glamorizing and giving tobacco more power over your life than it actually has. I believe you already have the desire to quit. Having a desire is unfortunately not enough to quit. You must instead develop a strong negative emotion associated with all tobacco products. An essential point to realize is that objects, events, and people do not make us happy or miserable. Our happiness or lack of it comes from within, not from external things.

It is the mind that interprets the emotion. You have to stop blaming others, situations, and conditions for your addiction, or using the power of nicotine to solve your problems. You don't enjoy smoking. How could you? Are you incapable of helping yourself? Do you actually believe that nicotine can bring peace, happiness, and meaning in your life? Nicotine may have the ability to calm your nerves, but this is only temporary. It does not solve your problems, but instead it adds problems. Therefore, you need to make a choice to quit, and to quit with this book. Waiting for the optimal time in your life is only an excuse. Fear is self-generated. We delay quitting because of the fear of withdrawal, weight gain, added stress, the addiction, and other reasons, but these notions are in your head. It is the lack of confidence in yourself that holds you back, not the addictive powers of nicotine.

Most people who are addicted to a substance are fearful. It is the vow to yourself to quit that will help you remain a nonsmoker.

The will to quit needs truth and understanding. The will works together with the soul and the heart. Some people can have the desire and the willpower, but their soul is damaged or feels deprived. Realizing the soul's needs and accepting it helps the soul, along with the will, give yourself enough drive to succeed where you have failed before.

It is true that we are all, in some ways, addicted to something, be it sports, TV, money, shopping, success, promotion, food, or sex. We check our cravings and attempt to put an end to the worst. Addiction is part of human nature, but we as humans must also be able to differentiate between those addictions that could possible kill us, such as smoking, and helpful ones, such as exercising.

Our urges sometimes seem to flow toward destructive forces of natures. The sinful things in life just seem more enjoyable. The problem with tobacco products is that they simply have no advantages. The disadvantages are so immense, how can you question whether you should quit and when? It is not important how many times you failed before. Just don't abandon hope. You might have fallen back into smoking again, after your New Year's or birthday resolution. So what? Get over it and start over again.

Learn to never surrender to something that is extremely, crucially important in your life. Allowing yourself to be defeated will cause you more damage to your soul than you know. All you have to do is believe in yourself and your inner power to change—to change even when your mind tells you that you don't need change. This is power!

Today we have become a community that looks for the easiest, fastest, and simplest approach to our problems. We take pills to help us concentrate, pills to make us feel less depressed, pills to help us stop eating, pills to help us be more sociable, pills to get us aroused—you name it and there is a pill for it.

Now, I am not saying that there is no need for *medication* in some incidences, but we have forgotten about *meditation*, and the power of the mind, and the power of prayer. Believe in yourself and know you can do it, and you will achieve your goals. Promise yourself you will not submit. Your life is too important to let a cigarette habit destroy you. The mind is a powerful, wonderful thing. As I mentioned before, you have the ability to control your urges.

As humans, we have many urges and desires everyday, but we don't always act on them. This is what separates humans from animals. Remember this every time you get the urge to smoke: Are you in control or not? If we all acted on our urges and desires, we would not exist as a civilization.

We can change our destiny. Am I saying that you can change your genetic makeup, if some day proof emerges of a smoking or an addictive gene with the power to keep one hooked on a habit? Yes, that is exactly what I am saying with relation to addictions and smoking. The simplest of organisms in nature can change its DNA code, to suit its environment. Viruses, bacteria, and many organisms have the ability to change their genetic structure to survive. Their genes mutate toward positive and beneficial order. Scientists have labeled this ability as random and chaotic. However, I believe that there is order and intelligence in chaos. Viruses, for example, change their protein and genetic makeup to become resistant to our attempts to kill them. This is why bacteria can become immune to antibiotics, and viruses are sometimes impossible to combat, such as the AIDS virus. Man is as only as good as the tools he possesses; this applies to woman, too, of course.

Science has dictated that once you have genetic flaws, it is almost impossible to change them, but there are higher elements of control. We as a scientific community have not yet discovered them. However, it just may be that we have not yet discovered the right tools to find them. For instance, remember the example that I gave you regarding the electron microscope where we could not imagine viruses until the invention of the tool that allowed us to see them. We could not see them with our simple light microscope. Thus, they did not exist until we discovered the tool to find them. The New Age movement speaks about these higher forces, the essence that ties us together. We cannot yet explain how the mind has the ability to do miraculous things, but it does.

The power of suggestion, or the power of prayer, works miracles. Don't look for the evidence to prove everything. We are not all-knowing beings. We do, however, have control over our thoughts and our actions. You are in control of yourself. All you have to do is believe that you can quit smoking and never go back.

Actually, at first you may have doubts. Ignore your doubts. You are all ready a nonsmoker. You can quit and never smoke again. Don't underestimate the power of your mind. You can do it this time! Remember that your past has nothing at all to do with your future. You know, deep down inside, that you want to quit. You told yourself that one day when the conditions are right, you would just quit smoking. You have put it off 'til next week, your next birthday, New Years Day, the new millennium; many smokers promised themselves they would quit in the year 2000. What happened? Why do you continue to smoke? Let's examine again some of the excuses.

CHAPTER 28

Why I Can't Quit

Excuse #1

I can't quit now because I have to concentrate, and smoking keeps me focused. I seem so confused when I quit.

We already know some data exists to suggest that smoking may improve concentration. There is also some evidence that it may actually lower your threshold of annoyance, therefore giving you a better environment to focus. Remember, there is always a flip side. Tobacco smoke has four thousand-plus chemicals, which enter your body every time you smoke, and many of these chemicals are known carcinogens. Tobacco byproducts such as carbon monoxide and cyanides deplete necessary oxygen to your brain and cells within your body, therefore robbing it of oxygen.

Temporarily, smoking may increase your awareness, but so do cocaine, LSD, and other stimulants. This does not mean they are good for you. In the long run, smoking will cause permanent damage to every cell in your body until it kills you. The short-term relief is not worth it!

Excuse #2

Quitting smoking is just too difficult!

This is true for some, but not for you anymore. You have no other choice but to choose health. Life is difficult, and the most rewarding things in life are usually difficult to accomplish. You have bought the best book on the market to help you rebuild yourself inside, in order to gain control of your actions and thought, in order to Nic Your Habit permanently. You have all the necessary requirements to quit forever. You have my Web site on which there will be lots of links and support to help with those difficult moments. In America alone, over three million smokers quit each year. You can too. Have faith in yourself!

Excuse #3

I have cut back—I smoke a new brand lower in nicotine and tar.

Using lower tar and nicotine cigarettes is actually worse for you. When you smoke such cigarettes, you are being fooled. Studies show that smokers tend to inhale deeper and smoke more. The amount of tar and nicotine in your blood can be twice as high as regular-brand cigarettes. In reality, you are not only increasing the amount of tar and nicotine in your body, but you are also increasing the level of other chemicals from tobacco smoke.

Excuse #4

Smoking relaxes me, and I just can't quit now.

This is caused by the nicotine effect on your body. It causes bio-chemical changes within your body, as all drugs do. You therefore become dependent on nicotine and begin to feel hopeless without it. Do you see the pattern? The fact is that nicotine is actually a stimulant that raises your blood pressure, along with your heart and breathing rates. In reality, after a month or so after quitting, you will without a doubt feel less nervous than you ever felt before. You are addicted and dependent on a substance. Please know this and believe that there is a better life after quitting. It just takes some time for your body to cleanse itself of the memories of your habit.

Excuse #5

There is too much happening in my life to quit! I'll quit later.

Some claim there is too much stress in their lives now, while others say they will quit when the time is just right. I must tell you that the perfect time will never come. There will always be stressful moments in your life, so the decision to quit smoking will just be postponed more and more, until you realize you must make the decision to quit and just do it.

Do you actually think you will wake up one day and not be a smoker? It doesn't work that way. You need to decide that smoking is wrong for you, and that you have had enough!

You do not need your life to be in perfect order to quit a habit. There is no magic pill or patch, and there are no magical sayings. Belief that you can do it is all you need. Just realizing that when you smoke, you poison your blood with substances from tobacco smoke is all you need to quit.

You may think that I am repeating myself, and this is true. I am repeating myself in this book to hopefully reprogram your mind, so that you won't forget that when you smoke, you allow carcinogenic pollutants and free radicals to penetrate every cell and organ within your body. Knowing all you have learned after reading this book and not deciding to quit would be a sad horror. Who in their right mind would pay for a drug from which one gets no benefit and which has the potential to kill you before your time? But in case you still have not gotten the message about how dangerous smoking is, here we go again …

CHAPTER 29

The Dangers of Smoking

According to the World Health Organization (WHO), tobacco use is reaching epidemic proportions. More than three million deaths each year are attributed to smoking. There are more than four hundred thousand deaths in America alone that can be prevented by not smoking. Just by quitting, you decrease your chances of acquiring one or more of these illnesses.

Smokers are not the only ones harmed by the poisonous effects of smoking. According to the American Heart Association (AHA), they estimate forty thousand people die each year from heart and blood vessel disease caused by secondhand smoke. The American Cancer Society reports that annual deaths related to secondhand smoke caused by heart, lung, and other diseases result in fifty-three thousand deaths annually. Sadly, these numbers are increasing. Secondhand smoke-related illnesses have become the third leading cause of death in the United States, after smoking and alcohol use. Knowing this, I truly hope you stop smoking around children and loved ones. I realize why it is illegal in many states to smoke in public places. Who wants to die from someone else's habit? Everyday, there is new research about how damaging smoking is to our whole body, but most people just don't care, or refuse to believe the facts.

Tobacco companies have known all along (for several decades) how dangerous smoking is to your health, and are making a lot of money from you through their lies, cover-ups, and diabolical actions to keep you addicted physically, mentally, and emotionally. Get out of denial. Don't be taken advantage of. It doesn't take a brain surgeon to realize that smoking is harmful. The chemicals within the tobacco smoke are poisonous and carcinogenic. Let me just refresh your memory about some of the chemicals found in tobacco products:

- Acetone (nail polish remover)
- Arsenic (rat poison)
- Butane (cigarette lighter fluid)
- Cadmium (rechargeable batteries)
- Carbon monoxide (car exhaust fumes)
- DDT (insecticides)
- Hexamine (barbecue lighter)
- Hydrogen cyanide (Gas chamber poison)
- Lead (paint and alloys)
- Naphthalene (mothballs)
- Nicotine (insecticide)
- Tar (used for all the chemicals within cigarettes that are not gaseous, non-nicotine, and non-water)

CHAPTER 30

One Hundred Reasons Why!

1. Because you can!
2. Quitting decreases the overall risk of death (all causes combined) by 50 percent in fifteen years as compared to continuing smokers.
3. Heart disease.
4. Stroke.
5. Arteriosclerosis.
6. Peripheral vascular disease.
7. More than one hundred of the four thousand-plus substances are known to cause cancer.
8. Cancer of the lung.
9. Cancer of the oral cavity.
10. Cancer of the throat.
11. Cancer of the esophagus.
12. Cancer of the pancreas.
13. Cancer of the kidney.
14. Cancer of the urinary bladder.
15. Cancer of the cervix.
16. Incidence of obstructive lung disease.

17. Chronic bronchitis.
18. Emphysema.
19. Other substances, known or suspected mutagens, that cause permanent, often harmful changes in the genetic material of living cells.
20. Smoking is responsible for more than fifty different medical conditions.
21. Women who smoke take longer to become pregnant and are more likely to miscarry.
22. Men who smoke may suffer impotence.
23. Smoking can affect sperm quality.
24. Women who smoke during pregnancy are more likely to have low-birth-weight babies.
25. Women who smoke give birth to babies who are premature, stillborn, or die shortly after birth—Sudden Infant Death Syndrome.
26. Toxic tobacco smoke, a.k.a. secondhand smoke, harms others.
27. Toxic tobacco smoke can cause asthma in your children.
28. Smoking reduces oxygen to the brain, thus may affect your mental function.
29. Smoking reduces your ability to perform in activities, such as sports.
30. You are paying big tobacco your hard-earned money to cause you harm.
31. Depending on where you buy cigarettes, you'll save more than $2,500 a year if you've been smoking a pack a day.
32. Smoking destroys your brain chemistry.
33. Smoking is a selfish drug and affects your personality for the worse.
34. Nicotine—a poisonous, addictive, drug, has been linked to cancer.

35. Nicotine is more addictive than heroine or cocaine.
36. Tobacco smoke contains four thousand-plus chemicals.
37. Smoking causes your breath to smell.
38. Smoking causes your teeth to yellow.
39. Smoker's cough.
40. Your sense of smell and taste will improve within days of quitting.
41. Fire prevention.
42. Increased work productivity.
43. Your family and friends will stop nagging you to quit.
44. You'll have more motivation to do the things that are really important to you.
45. Constant cough/sore throat.
46. Respiratory problems will decrease.
47. Gum disease risk.
48. Nonsmokers don't like kissing smokers. There is nothing sexy about smoking.
49. You won't feel like a leper in public. More than 70 percent of people don't smoke.
50. You won't have to lie about your addiction.
51. Frostbite in the winter would be a thing of the past. Your fingers and toes will thank you.
52. You won't have to go outside to smoke to get your nicotine fix.
53. Your pets will live happier and healthier.
54. You won't have to dry clean your clothes as much.
55. Every cell in your body will benefit.
56. Your house will smell better.
57. Your car will smell better.
58. You will be a winner because you finally took control of your addiction.

59. You will have a lot more energy.
60. You will contribute less to world pollution.
61. Tobacco smoke has ammonia in it.
62. Tobacco smoke has lead in it.
63. Tobacco smoke has hydrogen cyanide in it.
64. Cheaper life insurance.
65. It's never too late to quit.
66. Chose health over addiction.
67. Risk of anesthesia and post-operative complications are increased by use of cigarettes.
68. Fifty million Americans have already stopped smoking, so why can't you?
69. Because you know that you want to quit.
70. When you quit for twenty minutes … your blood pressure drops to near the level before you had your last cigarette.
71. After eight hours … the carbon monoxide level in your blood drops to normal.
72. After twenty-four hours … your chance of heart attack decreases.
73. After two weeks to three months … your circulation improves. Lung function increases up to 30 percent.
74. After one year … your chance of heart attack is cut in half.
75. After five years … stroke risk is reduced to level of a non-smoker.
76. After ten years of quitting, precancerous cells are replaced and cancers such as mouth, larynx, esophagus, bladder, kidney, and pancreas decrease.
77. After fifteen years off cigarettes, the risk of death for ex-smokers returns to nearly the level of persons who have never smoked.
78. Because you love yourself.

79. You want more control over your life.
80. No more going to the store in the rain or snow for your addition.
81. You can have sex longer without being out of breath.
82. Smoking has been linked to depression.
83. Smoking will not help you lose weight.
84. Children tend to imitate their parents.
85. Smoking makes no sense.
86. Your hair, clothing, and breath will no longer smell of cigarettes.
87. Not socially acceptable anymore.
88. Smoking interferes with hormones.
89. Birth control pills and smoking severely increases risk to heart attack, stroke, and blood clots.
90. Cigarette smoking appears to be a substantial risk factor for the development of diabetes.
91. Smokers are 1.5 times more likely than nonsmokers to suffer fractures, sprains, and other physical injuries.
92. Smoking increases blood pressure.
93. Smokers are three times more likely to get middle ear infections than nonsmokers.
94. Smoking is a major factor contributing to the early development of age-related macular degeneration.
95. Smoking decreases a man's chances of maximizing the full potential of his erect penis.
96. Smoking damages blood vessels, inhibiting blood flow.
97. Smoking destroys brain cells and prevents others being produced.
98. Smoking activates genes that cause skin to wrinkle.
99. You don't need any more reasons to quit.
100. Quit for yourself.

I could go on and on about all the harmful substances in the tobacco smoke, but that would be useless. I dedicated a whole chapter in this book to the harmful effects of these chemicals, so when science finds new evidence regarding the effects of tobacco upon our body, don't be surprised. How could you be? How can smoking cause anything but harm to your body with all of those harmful toxins and poisons present in tobacco products?

Tobacco companies and advocates for smokers claim that the amounts of these substances in tobacco smoke are minuscule and vary from time to time. Hey, if you can measure it, then it is way too much for me. I'll pass on ingesting the rat poison, insecticide, mothball, lead, and arsenic. Obviously, the tobacco companies would try to convince you that smoking is safe. They are selling a product! I am telling you they are lying to you.

The cells within our body are extremely sensitive, not only to the amount of substance, but also to the electromagnetic radiation of the substances in tobacco smoke. Our body is also sensitive to change and foreign matter. We are not only made of substance, but also of energy. The smallest amount of substance can have extremely damaging effects to the cells in our body and to our electrochemical self, especially over prolonged duration. Who would have ever thought that the sound waves from your cell phones, microwaves, television, computers, and even electrical power lines could cause your body harm? There is some evidence that prolonged exposure to electromagnetic radiation can cause cells to go out of control.

Do you actually believe that the four thousand-plus chemicals found in tobacco smoke have no actions on your body?

Cigarette smoking is known to be the major cause of preventable deaths in America. Hopefully, you will choose health over death by quitting smoking and never touching another tobacco product again. If you quit before you come down with a smoking-related illness, your body has the ability to completely restore itself. Please remember, when you smoke around others, you are also jeopardizing their health.

My sister, who has never smoked, was told at the age of thirty-nine by her doctor that her chest X-rays showed patterns of a smoker. Her lungs were not those of a thirty-nine-year old woman, but more like those of a fifty-year-old smoker. For over fifteen years, she had been exposed to tobacco smoke in her workplace; just working in smoke-filled rooms had caused serious damage to her lungs. She was outraged! She would always complain when I smoked around her, and I never listened, but instead continued to smoke, especially when she visited me in my home—*how selfish of me!*

There is new evidence that even after a room is cleared of tobacco smoke, the harmful effects of chemicals remain and linger in the air. If you are still smoking, you must start to think about seriously quitting. Some of you might have already had enough and already quit, but remember, if you do quit before finishing this book, you must read it to the end. For those still somewhat reluctant to quit don't worry. There is a section where you will say goodbye to all tobacco products forever. Right now, I hope you have made a commitment to not smoke around others, even if they give you permission. Remember that every time you smoke in the presence of another, you are potentially harming that person with the fumes from your cigarette. These fumes are poisonous to their lungs and every cell in their body, just as they are to you.

You don't have to believe this statement, because if you are still smoking, you are probably already in denial. Why harm others with your cigarette smoke? Just don't do it, especially around children. It would be like giving a child drugs. If you are an intelligent person, then you must realize that all reasons you continue to smoke—after knowing that smoking is so dangerous—are just excuses.

Studies have found a strong cancer-causing chemical called NNK, which has been detected as NNL-Glu, the metabolized product, in the urine of nonsmokers. If NNK is only found in tobacco, how can this substance get into the urine of nonsmokers? The only way is from the smoke of others that is absorbed into their bodies by being in smoke-filled rooms. Secondhand smoke is a reality. It doesn't require you to believe the research for it to cause harm.

The Switch

Now that we have talked about the reasons you should quit and how dangerous smoking is, I want you to concentrate on realizing that you need to give up your habit. First, we are going to start by switching cigarettes. Either toss away your packs or carton of cigarettes in your home or office, or trade them for a different brand. If you smoke menthol, I want you to switch to nonmenthol—the brand doesn't matter, the important thing is the switch. And if you usually smoke nonmenthol, I want you to switch to a menthol cigarette. If you like, you can smoke *one last cigarette* from your favorite, current brand, *but smoke only one cigarette.* This will be the last cigarette from your favorite brand that you will ever smoke. So enjoy it …

And now, since you have had your last drag of smoke from your favorite brand, from this point onward, you must smoke the new brand. This is one of the most important exercises in this book. While you are smoking the new brand, I also want you to think about being a nonsmoker—even if you don't believe it. While you taste the (menthol/non-menthol) taste, think to yourself about how horrible smoking is for you and your health. Soon, you will no longer smoke at all. Close the book now please, don't continue reading until have smoked a couple of cigarettes from your new brand.

CHAPTER 31

The Withdrawal Symptoms

Quitting does come with withdrawal symptoms. Some of the experiences that I have encountered were similar to losing my best friend. I felt depressed, lonely, and agitated, not knowing how I would manage in life without cigarettes. I felt irritable and totally stressed out. These were just a few of the psychological withdrawal symptoms that I experienced. You may also experience headaches, sweating, nausea, the shakes, and nervousness. Or you may not experience any withdrawal symptoms at all; some people don't. But whatever you go through, the symptoms last only four days.

Because of my irritability and being a total jerk to all who knew me, such as family and friends, some of them wished I would go back to smoking. I would pick fights for no reason. At work, I was a total mess. I could not focus or concentrate. According to a research study that I read, the average smoker with such mood swings tends to go back to smoking within two weeks. It was so difficult for me, since I smoked three packs of cigarettes a day. At the first couple attempts, I would last for a month or two, and then something would go wrong in my life and I would start smoking again. What was I thinking? Smoking did not have the ability to help me with my problems. I needed to learn how to relax and cope. This is something that one learns from therapy or through meditation, not by cigarette smoking, or eating, or drugs, or alcohol.

I was lucky to be in another country when I finally quit for life; I was on vacation in a spiritual environment and I was silent. This was my solution. I just kept to myself. You are luckier, since you have all the solutions to quit, here in this book.

To sum up, you may experience some symptoms, or none-to-a-few, depending on the stresses in your life, and how you feel about yourself when you decide to quit. In Nepal, when I felt depressed and needed that chemical rush, I hiked the Himalayas or jogged through the mountain range. I did what I had to to keep my mind occupied. I knew that I would never return to cigarettes, but I had horrible withdrawal symptoms. Don't let this scare you, the reward is far greater.

Some known withdrawal symptoms include:

- Depression
- Loneliness
- Irritability
- Stress
- Feelings of helplessness
- Difficulty concentrating
- Headaches;
- Sweating
- Sleep disturbances
- Nausea
- Intense cravings for cigarettes
- Intense craving for food and fluids

This book is about truth, self-awareness, and trust. I won't lie to you. It will be difficult for some. Everything that is important in life is difficult. If you need to take time off work for two days or so, then do it. This may scare you and put you off quitting even more. You may tell yourself that you can't cope with going through all of these withdrawal symptoms right now, but you *can* do it! If I can do it, then so can you. I hate pain and I don't like to suffer, but I made up my mind and decided that I was going to quit and nothing was going to stop me.

Quitting smoking will bring a bit of discomfort to your life, but it's nothing to worry about. If you care about yourself and those who love you, quitting smoking is one of the smartest decisions you can make. In just three or four days, the cravings will just stop. You will still have the habit and the emotional addiction, but the physical addiction will be gone.

You will handle your emotional addiction through control and your desire to remain a nonsmoker. You will also not return to smoking because you know how damaging smoking is to your health, and you can now look at others who still smoke and feel proud that you have finally kicked the habit. Your craving for cigarettes will be overcome by your disgust of cigarettes. You gain so much from quitting. The habit will be the only thing you need to work with. The thoughts of having a cigarette while on the phone, after dinner, during coffee, lunch, or your break, will cause you to want a cigarette. Hang strong and fight the urge, and just say no. Don't allow a cigarette to control you! You are stronger than that. You will notice the difference in becoming a nonsmoker.

Assignment # 4

For this assignment, you will need a glass jar with a lid, such as a large pickle jar, that can hold at least two cups of water. If you don't have one in the house, please go out and buy one. This will be used as your ashtray from now on. Now I will ask you to commit. I want you to go through your home and office and throw out every ashtray you own. It doesn't matter how much you paid for the ashtrays, or if they were a gift to you, or how sentimental they are to you. This is the first important step to the road of becoming a nonsmoker. You may think how wasteful it is to discard your ashtrays. You may want to give them to a friend or family member. But if you have been reading this book, you know that by no means should you give another smoker your ashtray(s); this would only support their addiction to tobacco products.

When I did not have all the knowledge I am presenting to you in this book, and was on my third attempt to quit, my friend Maria, who is in the Air Force Reserves, came to my home for a Fourth of July pool party. She had just returned from Saudi Arabia and bought some Hefe-Weissen Bier from Germany, cigars from Saudi Arabia, and an expensive lighter from France, not knowing that I had quit smoking while she was away. Of course, she did not believe me because I had quit so many times before. She looked a bit disappointed, so I said, "Wait a moment, one cigar can't hurt me or get me back to smoking. It wasn't cigars that I was addicted to, but cigarettes. This is my party, so let's celebrate." I yelled out to my friends to come over and have a cigar with me. Everyone was so excited about trying a cigar from Saudi Arabia, even those who had never smoked cigarettes in their lives. Cigar smoking was in. Cigar magazines were flaunting just how elegant cigar smoking was by having celebrities on the cover, with tuxedos and evening gowns and a cigar in their mouth. I knew four women who began smoking cigars because they believe it to be glamorous.

You know the ending to this story. I made one mistake as a recovering smoker, which was to take another puff. I was dumb and stupid.

Nicotine was my addiction, and one puff of the cigar got me hooked again on my habit; it did not matter if I smoked a cigar, chewed tobacco, or smoked a cigarette. Nicotine is nicotine. In a matter of two weeks, I was back to my old ways, smoking one cigarette after the other. I was hooked again. One thing you must know is that once you stop smoking, you can never again smoke or use nicotine products … just like a recovering alcoholic who can never again touch a drop of alcohol.

Temptation will drive you mad with wanting to smoke a cigarette. Let your temptation be your newfound strength. Every time that you say no to smoking, you increase your power to control your urges. The best way to help with your cravings is to think just how horrible smoking is to your health. Think about all the toxins that you inhale with each puff. Take control over yourself and be strong! I am still disgusted by the smell of tobacco, and I also choose health over illness. I have built such a strong hatred for tobacco and everything associated with cigarettes, that I would never allow myself to be a slave again to tobacco and the poisons they deliver to my body.

This is an extremely important factor in becoming a nonsmoker forever. All the subliminal messages wrapped around positive images of smoking and tobacco products must be erased from your consciousness. This is why I am asking you to throw away your ashtrays. You will no longer have a need for them in your home or office, as they serve no other purpose. Keeping them would be the same as a drug addict saving his old needles and syringes after quitting heroin.

I know it may be difficult to throw away possessions that have memories attached or have cost a bit of money. It seems wasteful. I felt the same way when I threw out a beautiful ashtray I had purchased in Egypt. It was made from alabaster and an array of stones. It was beautiful, but I wanted to part with everything that kept me bound to cigarettes. I went as far as throwing away all items linked to tobacco products, including the lighter my dear friend had given me from Paris. I won't ask you throw out your lighters, because they have other purposes than lighting cigarettes.

Now that you have cleared away your ashtrays, you are left with the glass jar, which will now be your ashtray. I want you to fill it with water, so that it is half full. When you smoke, I want you to empty your ashes into this jar, along with the butt of your finished cigarette. Then close the jar and put it somewhere nearby, where you will have it when you smoke. Use it until it is filled with cigarette butts and ashes. This assignment is to visually reinforce what is going into your body.

Now … before you light your next cigarette, you need to do a couple of things. Take a moment and think about all the chemicals and toxins in each cigarette you smoke. Look at the jar, then open it and smell the contents just before you light up again. Some may not want to smell it, but I say to you "Why?" Smelling it is not as bad as smoking it! The smell is enough to make you sick. This is all the junk and toxins you are putting into your body each day.

My main objective for you is to help build negative emotions around smoking, so before you light each cigarette, take a deep breath of your jar. This may sound like a dumb assignment, but it is not. Your mind needs this reinforcement. By reading this book and practicing the assignments, I want to stimulate all of your senses to come to a realization that smoking is really not a wise choice, and I want you to build negative emotions around smoking. Visually, you can see how disgusting the remnants of your cigarettes are. You can also smell how toxic these chemicals are. These inputs are important for you to undo the positive messages that keep you hooked on nicotine. Building these negative emotions toward cigarettes guarantees you will never go back. You can't quit successfully and still have positive feelings toward cigarette smoking.

CHAPTER 32

The Secrets to Quitting Smoking Forever

Smoking can kill. The research is available and I can provide thousands of citations in relationship to the evidence, but you already know this. This is common sense. Even if you ignore the claims of how damaging smoking is to your health, you still can't deny that smoking has a negative effect on you. Just go to your doctor and take a stress test. You will have all the proof you need.

You absolutely can't be in shape and smoke a pack of cigarettes a day for a year or more. We have seen, heard, and read the reports about smoking, and we are all well aware about the findings of smoking and cancer, yet we choose to deny or ignore them

Regarding the it-won't-happen-to-me-or-my-family syndrome. Why take the risks? Why pay your hard-earned money to tobacco corporations, with the hope that smoking won't take your life, or that you will somehow be spared? We hear stories about people who smoke until the age of ninety and are still going strong. This is hogwash! This person is not you and probably doesn't exist! Get real and admit the facts! This book may at times seem harsh, hard, crude, insulting, and occasionally rude, but it was written to spark your emotions to abhor cigarettes, thus enabling you to banish your need to smoke forever. Without emotions, there is no change. I want you to hate cigarettes. You absolutely can't have mixed emotions about smoking. You must know that it is dangerous. Tobacco products must be seen as your enemy. You must hate smoking and feel sorrow and disgust for smokers who continue to smoke. So many people give excuses about why they can't quit, instead of thinking of all the reasons why they should.

My sister-in-law blames her husband for her inability to quit. She claims that it is impossible to quit when someone in your home also smokes. This, of course, is also complete nonsense You are an individual and you have to be strong enough to not be influenced by others. This only shows weakness and lack of self-discipline! Get mad, so you can Nic Your Habit. You must develop a new consciousness around tobacco smoke.

I remember in college, my good friend Antonio quit and never smoked another cigarette. He quit once and never went back. I remember how annoying he was whenever I smoked around him. He could not be around tobacco smoke, even outdoors. I always wondered how an ex-smoker could be so negative about an act he had once enjoyed. I understand the reasons today.

I have another good friend, who hasn't smoked for fifteen years, and put his mother up in a hotel for a week, because he did not want her to smoke in his house. He did not even want anyone smoking outdoors on his property. He would always tell me that I was an idiot for smoking. When he found out that I started smoking again at my Fourth of July celebration, he stopped speaking to me and called me a loser. We had a big argument, and to this day we are still not speaking. This may sound a bit extreme, but it is not. I found out that he recently lost his father to lung cancer. So why should he have pretended to accept my addiction? Cigarette smoking and nicotine addiction killed his father, and he saw me going down the same road to killing myself with a cancer stick.

Smoking kills more people in the world than drugs. There is nothing nice to say about cigarette smoking. You must declare war on drugs in your life. It cost me more than four thousand dollars to go to another country to find myself so that I could quit. You now know everything you need to know in order to successfully quit smoking. It is up to you. I will repeat a few tips to help you quit, and stay a nonsmoker for the rest of your life:

1) You have willpower and you have control over your life.
2) You are strong and committed and have the power to do anything you want to do.
3) Smoking and nicotine have no control over you.
4) You have control over your mind, and your mind does as you say, not vice-versa.
5) You don't need to substitute anything for smoking.
6) You must learn to take control, not get another addiction. Some people substitute smoking with eating, drinking coffee, soda, alcohol, and chewing gum. Don't do it.
7) You should, however, buy extra fruit, vegetables, and drink as much water as possible to help cleanse your system. I joined a gym after quitting for the last time, and I started jogging five miles every other day. This is not possible for everyone, but if you are not physically limited, you should, without a doubt, increase your physical activities.
8) Walk more and exercise. Get yourself checked out by your doctor prior to engaging in any exercise program.
9) Please attempt to quit cold turkey without drugs or more nicotine products. Your mind is more powerful than any drug.
10) You can quit alone, using your willpower. Your mind is an incredible machine. What you feed it, it will relate. If you develop a disgust toward tobacco products, it won't allow you to smoke again. If you have mixed feeling about cigarettes, and those who smoke around you, then your mind will think it is okay to start smoking when you are stressed, can't concentrate, or are nervous, along with all the false beliefs that you learned to associate with smoking. Instead associate smoking with death, cancer, black lungs, yellow teeth and nails, bad breath, smelly clothes, hair, smelly house, poor health, addictions, etc.
11) Believe that people who smoke are nothing more than addicts who cannot take control over their life. Smoking is

abusive and destructive. Cigarettes can kill you and the ones you love, whether they smoke or not. Picture this! Hear it in your mind every time you crave a cigarette. Talk to yourself silently and aloud, every time you see someone else smoke. Say to yourself. "Look at this person who is smoking. He is an addict. How sad and disgusting. He wants to quit but can't." Associate the smell of cigarettes with poisonous gas and stay far away from it.

12) Don't tolerate it even if you feel comfortable around it. Remember, nicotine is your enemy. Even if you don't yet believe this, you must start to convince your mind that it is so.

13) You have the willpower to quit, and you can take control over your life. You are strong, committed, and have the power to do anything you want.

14) Smoking and nicotine have no control over you. You have total control over your mind! Your mind does as YOU say, not vice-versa. You don't need to substitute anything for smoking. You must learn to take control and just simply quit.

15) After quitting, some people try to satisfy the urge with other substances. Some substitute smoking with eating, drinking coffee, soda, alcohol and chewing gum. Don't do it. You may, however, eat extra fruit and vegetables, and drink as much water as possible to help cleanse your system. Vitamin supplements are also a good idea. I joined a gym after quitting smoking and started jogging five miles every other day.

16) Get yourself checked out by your doctor before engaging in an exercise program. Don't rush the physical activity. Just take it slow and one day at a time. I did the opposite. After I quit and saw how I had let myself get out of shape, I exercised like a maniac—treadmill, jogging, bicycling, running, jogging, and whatever I could do to get back into shape. No one has to have a body that they don't like.

17) Remember, you eat to nourish the body, not to satisfy it. Don't eat until you are full. It will take a while for you to adapt to this concept, but it is worth it.
18) Take back your life. Control your urges, no matter what your history is. Change your destiny now and just do it!

Assignment # 5

I want you to start analyzing smokers, as well as *your* smoking habits and patterns. Notice how they light their cigarette, notice which brand they smoke. Notice how they inhale and exhale. Notice whether they seem to enjoy their cigarette. Notice everything you can about them.

This time, I want you to analyze and make assumptions about their habit. I am asking you to judge only because I want you to get rid of the positives of smoking. This may sound like a double standard and it is. It is a terrible thing to look at others and notice their weaknesses. However, it is a wise man who learns from the mistakes of others, so that he does not have to experience their misfortune. Learning from others can help you grow. See how smokers light up a cigarette almost mechanically, immediately after they go outside.

I want you to think about the effects of smoking. Notice when others light up and think about all of the poisonous chemicals entering their body. Repeat to yourself how disgusting cigarettes are. After each cigarette you smoke, take only five puffs and throw it away with a feeling of disgust. If at home, put it into your nasty jar, or outdoors, step on it and say to yourself, "I hate cigarettes!" Do this each time you smoke. Now you have your assignment for the day. Do this for the entire day and night. Some of you may have already stopped smoking because you just couldn't stand the switch. Some of you may have never done the switch. That is okay.

Please take a day off from reading this book. Close it for twenty-four hours or so, then resume on the next page …

Remember you can do it. You will be a nonsmoker, even if you feel you can't. You can! Remember, take hold of your past so you don't relive your mistakes. I did it and have taught many others the same techniques offered in this book, and they are still nonsmokers today. In this book I stressed developing a strong hatred for all tobacco products. This is exactly what you need. Hate and loathing of tobacco products will keep you from ever going back. Anything less won't cut it. I have given you a lot of information. All the stories and references are essential to building you up to understand what nicotine is and what tobacco products can do to you.

Let's go over some of the key elements in this book:

1) Gaining insight into yourself through self-awareness;
2) Nonjudgment;
3) Meditation;
4) Understanding your emotions;
5) Realizing your addiction;
6) Recapturing your first experience with smoking;
7) Realizing the chemicals within tobacco smoke;
8) Understanding how you got hooked: the tobacco companies' propaganda;
9) The effects of nicotine, and how it is actually a drug that alters your brain chemistry and keeps you hooked to your habit;
10) Building a hatred for tobacco products;
11) Learning how to be real with yourself;
12) Get out of denial;
13) Stop being destructive and choose what is right;
14) Don't be stubborn, you know what is right;
15) Finding your spiritual self through God, meditation, and quieting the mind;
16) Choosing health over illness through quitting smoking;
17) Courage and faith in yourself.

CHAPTER 33

Time to Say Goodbye!

You are not giving up anything when you quit smoking. You are instead regaining control of your life, a new life of health and clear lungs, along with new vitality. You have learned a lot of new information, and you have succeeded in making it to this point in the book. Congratulations, I am truly happy for you. Deciding to quit smoking forever is one of the most important decisions of your life, as smoking affects so much of your world.

This is the section in the book where, if you haven't quit already, now is the time to say goodbye forever to tobacco.

Take a deep breath. And now take another one. Now. Not tomorrow. Not in an hour. Not after another cigarette. Smoking is over for you. You have smoked your last tobacco product.

Get your cigarette packs and cartons. Please gather them all. You have smoked your last tobacco product. Take whatever is left to the sink and destroy them with water. Turn on that faucet and watch them soak.

If you are at work, go to the staff bathroom and do the same. And you must do the same when you go home. You no longer need cigarettes. Take a deep breath, and another one, and go to it—soak those butts! Do it, and go on to the next page. Go ahead!

CHAPTER 34

Congratulations!

You are a nonsmoker. I truly hope you destroyed all your cigarettes. Remember what I told you about being stubborn and denying what you know is best. You know you have wanted to quit smoking for some time now. I helped you along and educated you, but only you are strong enough to quit.

It is easy to read this book and find fault with it, so you don't have to quit. You can then feel comfortable for again not listening to your spirit … Stop procrastinating and just quit! If you haven't destroyed all your cigarettes, here is another chance. Go ahead. You are the only one who can take control over your thoughts. Don't play tough with your health. Be tough when taking control over your life. You can do it because millions of people do it each year and so can you.

I have developed a Web site to help you and bring you supporting information to continue on your smokeless journey. On my site, you can find many links to other sites to help you stay a nonsmoker for the rest of your life. If you don't have access to the Internet at home or work, most public libraries now have free Internet access.

The "Nic The Habit" website is:

http://cigarettesmokingkills.com

CHAPTER 35
Recommendations

Withdrawal symptoms may kick in, and you will start feeling nervous, irritable, or unable to focus and concentrate. You may even get flu-like symptoms. So what? If you feel sick, then take the day off from work or school. You have a real addiction, and quitting smoking is no joke. It is difficult, but it is also easy. It is nothing more than forbidding you to succumb to your urges, so be strong and confident that you can do it. Your mind will naturally try to cause you to revert to your old ways, and will do everything possible to get you back to smoking. This is why people stay addicted. You will have many thoughts, emotions, and urges to smoke again.

Remember, your mind will attempt to combat your new insights and control you. Don't forget you have ultimate control over yourself. Tell you mind's thoughts to "shut up" or simply tell yourself, "stop." You can tell your mind every time you have the urge to smoke, to stop it! Say you are a nonsmoker and choose health, and that you will never go back to smoking. This is one trick to control your mind. It may sound weird or strange giving your mind commands, but it actually works. It is called mind control. Your mind listens to what you feed it and will respond with actions.

Drink plenty of water and juice. I can't stress this enough. When I quit smoking, I would drink water every two hours.

Whenever I had the urge to smoke and it became unbearable, I drank water and ate pickles. Pickles are great and are also low in calories. But for those who should limit their salt intake, pickles are not the best choice.

Now, your urge won't disappear right away. But, you can handle it. You have all that it takes, and much more, to never smoke again. Try to avoid caffeine products. Coffee, some teas, and sodas contain caffeine and can sometimes trigger your mind to crave nicotine. Enjoy the fresh air, go out more, walk, and enjoy life as a nonsmoker. I am proud of you and you should be proud of yourself.

And if you weren't quite able to quit this time, that is okay too. Wait a few days, think about quitting, then start from the beginning, follow the directions, and try again. *YOU CAN DO IT*!!

When you go outdoors, take a slow breath into your nostrils and a slow breath out through your mouth. Your whole body will benefit. It is also essential to exercise. Exercise will get those natural endorphins to rise and will help you get over the physical addiction faster. I can't stress exercise enough, but do it safely and with the advice of your health professional.

Continue with the meditation. Just before you go to bed, repeat to yourself that you are a nonsmoker finally free from all the toxins associated with tobacco. Perform visualizations of yourself in situations where you would normally smoke but don't. For instance, imagine that a friend offers you a cigarette, and you really have an urge for it. See yourself in your mind's eye saying, "No, I don't smoke." Don't say thank you or indicate how long ago you quit. Just say, "I don't smoke," and leave it at that. Do these visualizations for three months. Remember, the meditative visualizations take only five to ten minutes.

For your first week, avoid friends who smoke, as they sometimes are not supportive to your needs and can be negative by intentionally offering you a smoke, to test you. You can't allow any setbacks! At my Web site, there are also hypnotic/subliminal tapes that you can buy to help with your meditation.

CHAPTER 36

The Last Assignment

Never use any tobacco product again.

This means not even just one puff.

I have faith in you, and you will do it this time.

Remember, your actions have consequences. If you continue to ignore the facts that cigarette smoking will one day cause you harm, you will be a victim. Just a day after the manuscript for this book was completed from the editor, my mother, Eris, passed away on January 30, 2004. Eris lived a beautiful life, but instead she chose to ignore her health. When you choose to ignore health there will be consequences. My mother had four years of pure hell. She was in and out of hospitals and suffered from high blood pressure, diabetes, and being overweight. She had five strokes, developed chronic lung failure, cellulitis, kidney and renal failure, and other complications. She even had to have her leg amputated due to her diabetes. Don't ignore your health! Be strong! Take control of your addiction. If you don't, your addiction will take control of your health as it did with my mother.

ABOUT THE AUTHOR

Joe Weaver was born in New York City. At the age of twelve, Joe became very interested in philosophy, spirituality, and religion. At sixteen, he would visit different ashrams in upstate New York, where he practiced yoga, reflexology, herbology, and meditation.

Joe studied biology at the State University at Stony Brook, New York, where he received awards for excellence in biological research. After graduating, Joe went to Tulane University in New Orleans, to participate in a research project, which was later published in the European *Journal of Pharmacology*, March 1993.

In 1994 Joe went to Germany to study medicine as an exchange student. Eighteen months into the program, he had a change of heart towards medicine and moved back to the United States.

Back in the United States, Joe noticed that he was losing his spirituality, and he did not like the "new" Joe that he saw. He was smoking more than three packs of cigarettes a day and was eighty pounds overweight.

At an attempt to rediscover his lost soul, Joe traveled to Egypt, India, Nepal, and Tibet to find himself. The result of his journey was the book *Nic The Habit*, a spiritual approach to quitting smoking without gaining weight." The second edition is *The Tao of Quitting Smoking*. Since the first edition, Joe has helped thousands of people quit smoking and has lectured in malls, bookstores, and colleges throughout New York City about the dangers of smoking and secondhand smoke. Joe also won the 2002 American Cancer Society's Great American Smoke-out Award, for leadership in building a smoke-free environment in New York City.

Printed in the United States
26324LVS00006B/65

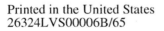